SARMADA

Fadi Azzam

Translated from the Arabic by Adam Talib

ARABIA BOOKS
LONDON

First Published in 2011 by Swallow Editions

This edition first published in Great Britain in 2011 by

Arabia Books
70 Cadogan Place,
London SW1X 9AH

www.arabia-books.co.uk

Copyright © Fadi Azzam 2011

Translation copyright © Adam Talib 2011

ISBN 978 1 906697 34 1

Typset in Minion by MacGuru Ltd
info@macguru.org.uk

Printed and bound by CPI Group (UK) Ltd, Croydon, CR0 4YY

A CIP catalogue for this book is available from the British Library

To Adad & Rina

I was born in Syria, in a village called Taara near the city of Suweida.

We didn't have electricity in the village until I was seven, but I've understood the value of light ever since. I first learnt to write in lamplight and so letters seem to me to shine even as the world grows dark.

I learnt everything important in life by the time I was seven years old: the meaning of light, nature, what it meant to be born innocent. All of that before the grind of school, party, and sect. Letters and words were the only things that could fly me up over the walls of these confines, and as I near forty, it seems not much has changed.

Words make us free. Anytime a place or a period of time goes wrong, the suffering turn to words. Words console, they give hope. I know their value because I grew up in a dazzling darkness. *Sarmada* is part of that darkness though it was written in the flicker of a white candle and the faint light of a lamp.

As words grow, space narrows, and as ideas expand, words fail to stretch. I felt I had no choice but to leave the most mysterious place I've ever known. That was Damascus.

I moved there when I was only eighteen, desperately seeking love, freedom and life. And it took me a decade of living in Damascus to realise that it's the only place on earth that doesn't care about passing time. It's puzzlingly steady. Everyone runs and hurries, wars and emigrates, but she simply waits for them to return.

No matter where you end up, Damascus is there waiting for you.

It's a mind-blowing and captivating city, cocooned in magic. You've got to fall in love, go to jail, go hungry and hang about before Damascus will give you the keys to its secrets. Otherwise it'll just carry on, content merely to be the oldest inhabited capital in the world.

When the brief Damascus Spring collapsed in 2001, I moved to Dubai.

It's the total opposite of Damascus. Dubai is a city of fantasies. Damascus is a fantasy city.

But Dubai gave me a passport to other cities: to London, Amsterdam, Lisbon, Prague, even to Paris, where in the drizzling autumn, on some side street, I met a woman who combined the darkness of Suweida, the light of Damascus, and the fancy of Dubai. We got married and she led me to a place where I could settle down. And then came *Sarmada*. Born out of the wombs of fertile cities. And my son, Adad, too, has been born – a second baby – as I watch my country struggle to bring its own more beautiful child into the world. Syria is in labour and freedom draws near.

Fadi Azzam, 2011

Chapter One

Azza

There wasn't anything about her that caught the eye. To tell the truth, I didn't even notice her until my friend introduced me – in Arabic – to the man from Syria standing beside her. We exchanged a few pleasantries, the way two compatriots do when they meet abroad, with restrained good cheer, dubious of what lay behind the words. Then he asked me where I was from. 'From the mountains.' When he asked me whereabouts exactly, I said, 'Sarmada', and just as soon as the words 'a village called Sarmada' left my mouth, the woman turned to us as if what I'd said had had some impact on her. She addressed me, looking a little out of sorts, and apologised for butting in.

'Did you say you were from Sarmada?' she asked.

'Yes', I answered calmly, though slightly unsure of where this was going. 'Do you know someone from there?' I asked, trying to decipher the look in her eyes. She was in her forties, wearing a black dress, accentuated by beads of the same colour. There was a look of smouldering disbelief in her eyes, and her face had become stern, severe even, as she examined me. I smiled placidly.

'What are the chances of meeting someone from Sarmada in Paris of all places?' she said. 'Do you live here?'

'No, no. I'm just here on business – a quick trip. I leave tomorrow.'

'How are things in Sarmada? How's the village doing?' she asked, her stare softening.

'Things are good – but, to be honest, I don't go back very often. I live in Dubai …' I was interrupted by the sound of heady applause echoing from around the hall. The French media personality, in whose honour the Institut du Monde Arabe was throwing this reception, had arrived. The woman's voice faded away and one of those dapper older gentlemen walked over to her, shifting her attention from our conversation to the party at hand.

Before she left, she said, 'My name's Azza Tawfiq. Have you got a pen?' I felt at my pockets, but I couldn't find one. She borrowed one from the sedate, dapper old man, who was looking at me icily. She scribbled her phone number down onto a napkin and handed it to me, her seeking eyes teemed with words unsaid. 'Call me. It's important…', she said; her voice was swallowed up by the celebratory din. The hall was packed and everyone was speaking French, which I didn't understand. My friend was caught up in the proceedings, and so I slipped quietly away. I strolled along the river Seine, watching the boats pass and the traffic in the street, savouring the splendour of a stroll through Paris, as my mind began to fill with images of my own tiny hometown. How had that woman suddenly brought Sarmada roaring back into my thoughts? Empty nostalgia had never been able to get its claws into me before. I'd built up defences against it over the many long years since I'd left that empty place, where lives are crushed, that land of waiting endlessly for what never comes.

Sarmada had never been anything more than a hollow shell that I'd happened to pass through. My bitterest days were spent there, and it had saddled me with pain and fear and fading out. It had taken me years to get it out of me. And now, by the banks of the Seine, something new was flickering inside of me, bringing Sarmada back; or at least what little of it had remained: a few, dusty old faces and some bland memories. There was no special taste or flavour left to tempt you into reminiscing about anyone in particular. As my footsteps quickened, my head began to swirl with sudden crazed thoughts. Can a man ever truly reject the place he was born, try to disown it, to deny its afflictions? So that's how it started, and it was like sinking into mire.

By the time I got back to the Hotel Alba in Saint-Michel, it was past eleven. I packed, took a hot shower, and let sleep swallow me up. I woke up feeling unusually energetic after a night of strange sleep. I went down to reception, settled my bill, took care of a few visa formalities, and left my bag at the desk. Then I called her. The voice on the other end was thickly drowsy, and thoroughly feminine. 'It's Rafi Azmi.'

'Who?'

'We met last night at the reception for Alain Ghayouche and you said I should call you.' Something must have clicked because her voice suddenly came to life.

'Oh, yes! Hello. When can we meet? Where?'

'My plane leaves from Charles de Gaulle this evening, so now, if you're not busy.'

'No, fine. Where are you?'

'Café le Depart – St. Michel.'

'I'll be there in half an hour.'

It was my last day in Paris and I was off to Damascus to continue researching a documentary I was working on about *Building Bridges between East and West*. My work as a film-maker meant I had to travel all over the place to arrange interviews and scout out shooting locations, but luckily for me I'd managed to finish everything I needed to do the day before. I'd decided to cap the day off by meeting up with an old friend from university, who'd invited me to the reception where the woman and I had met.

We sat at a corner table opposite the Gibert Jeune bookshop. There was a severity, and a certain whispering sadness, in her big, brown eyes, and a fairly noble air seemed to overlay her features. She spoke Lebanese Arabic, and after no more than a few words of small talk, delved straight into the heart of the matter. 'I'm from the Chouf, and I've got relatives in Sarmada.'

'Right, well that explains everything', I said, and parried, 'So this is all just sectarian sentimentality?'

'No, it isn't that.' She was silent for a beat, and then she looked straight into my eyes and in all seriousness said, 'I lived in Sarmada in a past life. If you believe in transmigration, or if you've ever heard of it, you'll know what I mean.'

I didn't say anything. I was too shocked to say anything. Of course, I had been raised in a culture that considered the transmigration of souls to be a key part of everyday faith and loved to tell stories about transmigrators, from the childishly entertaining to the wilfully exaggerated – if only to underline the fact that a belief in metempsychosis made the Druze stand out from all the other esoteric sects, who believed in transference, or animal, vegetable and mineral transmutations. Transmigration is when a soul travels from one human being to another, and it's entirely distinct from those other beliefs – about the soul being transferred into the body of an animal, or into a plant, or the worst punishment of all, into a rock, which was only for the souls that would be the most tortured of all, bound and confined within a rock or a boulder, a kind of eternal punishment until it's decided that the soul should be freed from its rocky imprisonment.

Transmigration, one of many mysterious tenets of the Druze faith, gives the community a feeling of blood purity and unadulterated lineage because Druze souls only ever transmigrate into Druze bodies. Not once in my life had I ever given the topic the slightest thought. I just considered it to be one of the many charming religious spectacles that Syria takes such pleasure in. She continued undeterred, 'I was murdered at half past four in the afternoon on the first Tuesday in December, 1968. My name in that life was Hela Mansour. I can still remember a lot about that previous life and – if you're interested – a lot of the details of what happened in the last two and a half hours. I can see it all with perfect clarity as if it were only yesterday.'

I studied her face, my own mouth agape, and saw how her

expression became clouded as she told her disturbing story. 'I don't really know how to put this,' I said, 'but the truth is, I don't actually believe in transmigration, or in much else, for that matter – except reason and science. To me, stories of transmigration are just collective memory. People who think they're recalling a past life are just recalling some common occurrences.' I thought about telling her the joke about the overweight fortune-teller, but something about her look – and her patronising smile – stopped my detached logic in its tracks.

'Listen, Rafi,' she began. 'I teach quantum mechanics at the Sorbonne and I wrote a PhD thesis on the development of Chaos Theory – if you even know what that is,' she added mockingly. 'But here I am, and I'm telling you that I had a past life and that my brothers murdered me ... I wanted to ask you about them. To ask how they're getting on.

'In any case, scientific logic and my personal life are two different things as far as I'm concerned. I've never told anyone what I'm about to tell you now – or at least not like this – but as Einstein said, "If the facts don't fit the theory, change the facts."'

'Are you saying you've got a theory about transmigration?' I shot back with equivalent condescension.

'No, not hardly. My own pride and logic always rejected the idea of my past life, or metempsychosis. And plus, I can't prove anything empirically. But the truth's inside of me, I realise that, and it's there with me. I'm carrying two lives – at least – inside of me, but that doesn't bother me anymore: after this life, I've started seeing things more clearly, less black-and-white. After all, Einstein also said that "Imagination is more important than knowledge."'

My memory threw out another Einstein quotation – not to provoke her, but to give her something to contemplate: '"Reality is merely an illusion, albeit a very persistent one."'

'And in practice', she added grudgingly, 'a persistent illusion beats an idiot's imagination.'

I felt like someone was trying to dismantle everything I thought

I knew and send me back into the deep anxiety I'd escaped so long ago. I thought that God, religion and all that other hocus pocus would never be able to trouble me again. But she cut in on my own silent self-trial and called upon the genius of relativity to boot, conjuring him up with a mystic's fluency: "'As far as the laws of mathematics refer to reality, they are not certain, as far as they are certain, they do not refer to reality.'" I backed down in the face of such unanticipated resolve, and to be even more frank, I don't think anyone in the whole wide world would've been able to resist the assuredness and sadness in that lovely woman's eyes. I let myself listen to her story, holding my judgment for another time.

She asked about the village: about some people I knew, others I'd at least heard of, and a few I didn't know at all. Little by little, we recreated the village together. We told its story and called forth its characters in that Parisian café just over the road from the statue of Saint Michel himself. Our conversation was amiable, full of some unknown cheer. I genuinely needed her help to be able to see the village where I'd grown up, the place I'd abandoned years earlier, and which was now nothing more than a stifling confine I liked to visit every few years or so to see my family and what friends were still around and then to make a hasty exit. Six hours flew by and it was time for me to leave. I told her I'd be back in Paris soon to continue my work and I promised her that I'd go to Sarmada and get the answers she was looking for, and that I'd be happy to see her when I got back. She hugged me and kissed my cheek and we both felt as if we'd known each other for years. When she wished me a safe flight, I felt like I was saying goodbye to a relative.

Not once during the entire five-and-a-half-hour flight did the story of Azza Tawfiq leave my thoughts. I didn't believe a word of what she'd said, of course, but all the same it had left me with a trace of pity and grief that tempered my cool detachment and filled me with a warm and burgeoning affection. For the first time since I'd left Sarmada years ago, something was happening inside of me, a moment of brightness, of revealing, that made me feel as if I were someone else. I took out my notebook and began recording – 'writing' isn't the right word – Azza Tawfiq's story, or maybe it was Hela Mansour's, and I forgot all about my to-do list.

༄

I arrived in Sarmada.

I carried her story around with me. I made enquiries, compared, contrasted. The evidence I'd collected in the beginning didn't prove anything: Hela Mansour could have been Azza Tawfiq, but she could have been any other woman for that matter. For a whole week, I roamed around the village and through its ruins, trailing the story, collecting and comparing all the different versions. Azza's voice returned and I could hear her as she told her story. Her words echoing in those places, in the faces of men and women who were still alive after all those years. I prodded at their memories and told the story from the very beginning.

༄

On a Tuesday at noon just after a light shower of rain, I, Hela Mansour, returned to Sarmada from the southern road, my hands free of warts, walking just as I had thirteen years before when I walked down to the Salt Spring. I slowed down as I crossed Poppy Bridge and looked out over the valley stretched beneath me. My eyes surveyed the contours of the village and the houses, which hadn't changed much, and I steeled myself, determined to keep it together for those few moments before I'd have to face the others. I knew full well the law in these parts. The blood of any woman who married against the wishes of the Druze community was considered suitable only for holy sacrifice or permanent banishment. I hadn't cared much about the details when I ran off with Azaday at the age of eighteen. I left my five brothers to endure excruciating pain and a great deal of derision, but I'd answered the call of my heart, and run off, driven by an obscure pleasure laced with the thrill of delicious, fervent fear, and of breaking a hard-and-fast law that had been around for more than 900 years.

֍

'Hela Mansour…' Salama repeated the name as if he were suddenly seized by some deep sorrow. He was quiet for a while and then continued, 'She was the most beautiful girl in Sarmada – I can still remember how she turned every head in the street. Women would drag their children indoors and the old men would climb up to the roofs to get a look at her. The whole of Sarmada was smitten. We never thought they'd actually go through with it, but the look in her eyes told us we'd been wrong. She faced her death with her head held high; she didn't seem the slightest bit afraid. God have mercy on her and her father. She was one of a kind.' Salama launched into a detailed retelling of that winter day; some of what he said matched what Azza Tawfiq had told me in Paris, but my job was just to collect it all impassively.

I didn't want to see transmigration as real and I didn't want reality to start transmigrating. I knew full well that life constantly repeated itself, confined to its fixed orbit, impervious to any specific time, and that Sarmada – like all the other small towns of the East – was happy to look no further than itself and it never changed much, no matter how much time passed.

Azza Tawfiq's story appeared and disappeared as I compared it to the different versions I heard from the townspeople, sometimes they corroborated her version and at other times they diverged from it. I decided I wouldn't make any judgments. I knew my responsibility was to record it all down with a documentarian's professional fidelity, and yet some powerful intuition told me that something was out there waiting for me, far beyond the borders of my comprehension. After all, I thought I was at a safe remove, safe from the bad omen the story portended. What came next would prove me entirely wrong: my life left its customary course and set down a new, unmarked path deep into the murky thicket of the past and future, as the boundary between different periods of time faded from view.

To discover what had happened to Hela Mansour, I would have to throw open the doors of that locked room, as if to air it out, to dispel the damp and musty torpor which Sarmada gave off. One question loomed above the rest: Had I really been born here? Had I actually lived here?

All through the quarter century I had spent here, the overpowering urge to get away from that remote world had kept me from appreciating my reality in all its fullness. So I set about gathering up pictures plucked from that scene to help me put a story together, and in the meantime other stories were preparing to rise up out of the gloom.

When I compared the recollections I'd collected in the village to what I'd heard from the physics professor, the first scene began to form before my eyes. If I were the type of person who insisted on captioning every last thing, I would have titled this chapter: 'Winter 1968: After five years on the run, Hela Mansour returns to her village.'

She walked along calmly, her hands wart-free, and passed by the old houses with her head held high in that supercilious way she'd inherited from her father, who'd fought in the Great Syrian Revolt and was one of the most esteemed men in the village. She walked down the narrow alleyways between the stone houses and caught snatches of what the people were whispering about her. Sarmada looked on, clammy with anticipation.

'She's fearless,' murmured some of the women.

'She's not being brave, she just wants to rub it in,' a neighbour retorted. 'She should've come back quietly. There are still some young men in this village, you know.'

'May God teach her shame,' said another.

'Pray for us, Blessed Virgin.'

'Lord help us,' said one, making the sign of the cross.

'Praise the Lord for making her! She's prettier than ever.'

'Folks say he kicked her to the kerb like a dog once he was through with her.'

'Protect us, Lord.'

'Shame on them.'

'She deserves whatever she gets.'

The scattered whispers ran down the village streets to the old family house, which her brothers had abandoned after she'd run off. They'd moved to the outskirts of the village, where they lived in exile with their shame, consigned to live in a world of wary looks and bated breath. In the air, the whispers of onlookers were mixed with acrid fear as everyone awaited the end of this woman, who had shamed her family, besmirched her father's good name and proud legacy, insulted Sarmada and its ways, and managed to evade every lethal trap her brothers had set for her over the years, and now she'd decided to return simply to die.

The story's getting a little confusing – I can tell – and if you're not familiar with the details, you're probably slightly uncomfortable with where things are headed, so I'll let Azza Tawfiq take over. Let's return to her, sitting in Café le Depart on the day we met, and let's listen closely so that the music coming from the Latin Quarter begins to fade away. I studied her voice, her gestures, the way the words slipped out from between her full lips, her eyes as they overran with mystery and wonder, and then all of a sudden, she stopped. She asked the waiter to bring us another round of coffee and some sparkling water. Then she turned to me once more, and with a mix of compassion and indifference, she said, 'Tell me when you get hungry. Lunch is on me.'

We had a few hours still before I had to leave. Thankfully, I'd thought to pay the hotel bill and leave my luggage at the desk. I nodded because I didn't want anything to interrupt the sound of her voice. My entire body was set on absorbing every single word she said, locking it away in my memory for safekeeping, where I was automatically assigning it a shape, a person, a place, a reference until it formed a complete and parallel world. Calmly, warmly even, she carried on, describing the murdered woman's route through the village, as if it were all just a picture she could see right in front of her.

The house she described was one I knew very well. The mulberry tree that Nawwaf Mansour used to guard was one of the highlights of my illicit fruit filching escapades as a child, and it stood directly across from Farida's place. Oh, I should mention to you that Farida and her son Bulkhayr will be making an appearance in our story presently; it's a bit like a relay race actually, with one runner passing the baton on to the next.

Allow me to return to Azza as she tells us about Windhill, Hyena's Rise, Poppy Bridge and how the village looks in winter. How this elegant Parisian, with her authentic Lebanese accent, knew the names of these different spots and byways in a neglected village, overrun with oblivion, dust and tedium, was beyond me, but it did give me incomparable pleasure! There was simply no heart-rending joy equal to hearing her say all those names that I'd locked up in my memory. Some had gone missing, some had morphed, but here they were; it was as if we shared the exact same childhood memories. Nevertheless, I'll let Azza tell the story so that I can try to put off my own memories, which had suddenly been brought back to life, and imagine a Sarmada I'd never known before. With that hypnotic voice of hers, she described her past life and how she arrived at her family home, which was near collapse since her brothers had abandoned it in shame. They had withdrawn to the outskirts of the village, leaving their old house at the mercy of armies of ants, roaches, spiders and moths. The Physics professor described her arrival – or Hela Mansour's – as follows:

'I came to the ruins of the old house and walked through the gate made out of can steel that rust had all but eaten away. I looked at the walls. I missed every stone in the place. I could smell the scents of my childhood locked away in each one. I prayed to God they wouldn't come just yet; that they'd give me some time. I didn't want to die there. I was worried that some of my blood would spill down to the mulberry tree, my old childhood friend, my dream-companion. Me, my mother and the tree, we were the only women in a house full of men, full of manliness. My mother had been buried beside the tree even though everyone was against the idea of her being so far away from the family plot up at the Khashkha-sha cemetery. I couldn't stand the idea of my blood seeping down into the darkness for my mother to taste.

'The sight of the decrepit old tree and her withered, leafless branches made me sad. She seemed smaller somehow, like a senile old woman. Can you imagine what it's like to know that you'll be dead in an hour?

'What are you supposed to do in an hour?

'But to tell you the truth, you can make an hour last a lifetime. And that's what I did. I dug a hole in the muddy earth around the massive tree trunk about a half-yard deep and buried a copy of my will. The will wasn't important – I don't even remember what I wrote – but I felt that I needed to leave something behind, some trace, whether on the earth or underneath it. I buried my mother's silver bracelets, too, and a little bell, which had once hung around the neck of a cow that'd been my childhood friend and given me my first reason to grieve. I prayed to my parents' souls to forgive me and to forgive my brothers for what they were about to do.

'The funny thing is that, to this day, when I remember going to the house, I get upset because I didn't sweep up or water the plants. I didn't spare a thought for the camellias, the lilies or the tulips; I didn't prune the jasmine to bring it back to life.

'Of course, I had run off with a stranger years before. I had abandoned my family because I loved him. But the day I did it, it was just an accident, a passing fear or a desire – I don't know. I can't really remember, and I probably won't ever be able to explain it.

'My brother Nawwaf slapped me with that massive hand of

his. The shepherds had already told them that I'd been meeting Azaday in the northern orchards. They'd found us embracing, sharing a kiss – my first. My first kiss became a scandal that swept through the entire village. It was also my first slap; no one had ever hit me before. My brother took a step back when he saw the blood pouring out from my nose and covering my face. He was furious, but he let me go and stormed off.

'Mother had died by then and I was left in their care. I was the youngest, I was the only girl and I was spoiled. Every pore of my skin gave off the scent of their mother and they'd been more liberal with me than any other brothers in Sarmada. The day I was caught kissing a stranger and the news of the scandal spread throughout the village was a disaster for them. In Sarmada, you can keep anything a secret for as long as you want, no matter what it is – except for love. Love is a disgrace. I'm not talking about sex or about a physical relationship; everyone has a physical relationship of some form or other. As long as it stays purely physical, then there's no shame in it. But for whatever reason, when it comes to love and something brings it to the surface, inevitably it's exposed. It shoots out from wherever it starts, meets with universal disapproval, and finds its way onto every tongue.

'In the room looking out over the garden, I wept as the blood continued to flow out from my nose, while they debated what they were going to do to him. They were threatening either to kill him or merely to beat him up until he was all but dead and they'd taught him a lesson he'd never forget. I couldn't stand to see him tortured like that, so I knew I had to go and warn him. He was scared and confused, sure, but I knew he wouldn't have run away. I walked calmly over to the water bucket by the front gate and washed and combed my hair, which was tangled and matted with blood. I put my hair up in a ponytail, grabbed a small bag and stuffed a few trivial things in it – I haven't a clue, for example, why I put the cowbell in – and then I slipped quietly away. They paid no attention to me, distracted as they were with their shouting and rage. It never occurred to them that I'd dare to leave the house after a scandal like that.

'I listened to them improvising oaths, swearing on their honour, and I slipped out right behind them. All it would've taken was for one of them to turn his head to see me leaving, but they carried on bellowing. I walked unseen through Sarmada and I knew exactly where to find him. We'd got used to operating in secret and so we'd figured out where we could meet safe from prying eyes. It didn't take long to find him near the vineyard. We clung to each other. We were both terrified and I can remember seeing tears in his eyes. I begged him to leave the village right away. I told him my brothers were planning to kill him, or to make an example out of him, and there was no point in trying to fight them. I begged him to leave Sarmada and I promised to love him forever. He pushed me back violently and then he grabbed me by the shoulders. "I'm not leaving you," he said. "Either I die here or you come with me. Only death can keep us apart." He was shouting and swearing that he wouldn't move an inch, that he wouldn't leave without me. He was deadly serious, resolute, insistent. And he had the most beautiful angry eyes in the world.

'I embraced him and said yes. I melted into him. All I remember is giving myself to him body and soul, just as he'd given himself to me. All it took was a few drops of blood and my virginity was lost. I'd shed all my bonds now. It wasn't a whim or a moment of weakness, it was a reality I'd created for myself without ever knowing how. I lay in his arms, half-naked, coated in dirt and dust and pleasure. "Fine. I'll come with you," I said.

'We spent all those years in exile walking together. The road and the villages and towns we passed through ate away at our feet. We tried to flee the country and failed, but we never stopped walking on and on. The loveliest memory, the thing I'll never forget, is that we walked along together. After that day, I felt as if I'd been born to walk, but there was still a short distance I had to cross to reach my final – fated – destination. And so, after I buried my will, the cowbell and my mother's bracelets, I walked out of the house and headed towards them.'

જ્જ

Everything I'd managed to learn confirmed the fact that the day after she'd run away was a total nightmare for Hamad Mansour's five sons. The villagers had all gathered in the square, some to gloat at their misfortune, others offering to help, and the brothers stacked the Epistles of Wisdom, the Quran, and the Bible all on top of one another and swore a savage oath: they announced that their sister had run off with some hotshot – as they'd taken to calling him – and they swore that they wouldn't light a single fire, or receive a single guest, or pronounce a single word about village affairs, or even trim their beards until they'd slit her throat. Salama told me what it was like to watch the scandal unfold: 'The brothers made that oath to hide their shame and to put an end to all the dirty gossip in the village. People are ruthless when it comes to those who violate the accepted customs, and to anyone associated with them.

'Over the next five years, the brothers grew more and more isolated, and their beards grew longer so that you could barely tell them apart, and they themselves struggled to tell one day from the next. It was a strange sight to see them going around together dressed in the same clothes, the same faces hidden behind long beards, with the same gloomy look. They were serious about killing her. The only thing that mattered to them anymore was tracking her down and killing her.'

Father Elias, the priest, who managed to be both caring and thoughtful, hugged me and asked me how I'd been. Had I missed him? He'd been a kind of godfather to everyone in my generation. He'd baptised all the children in Sarmada and ministered to them all – Christian, Druze and Muslim – for they were all God's flock. Similarly, he insisted that the Christian boys in the village be circumcised like all the Druze and Muslim children in the village. He was known for his easy-going sense of humour and his ability to find something to laugh about in any situation no matter how bitter it was.

It had been customary in Sarmada for the villagers to have their children baptised ever since people had come and settled here from the Lebanon 300 years ago. It was both a religious and a social rite for everyone in the village, regardless of confession or sect although no one really understood how it managed to work. In civil-war Lebanon, people were killed based on their sect: they were raped with whisky bottles, their corpses were mutilated, their skulls were gouged with power tools and their throats slit with razor blades. The people of Sarmada, on the other hand, lived together peacefully. I'll never forget how in 1983 two families, one Christian and one Druze, escaped over the mountains from Lebanon and took refuge with relatives in Sarmada. Lebanon's sectarian thinking could never understand how a majority Druze village would consent to be led by a Christian! Or why the Christians in Sarmada would donate money to help build a majlis, the Druze house of worship!

They'd find it no less astonishing, of course, to know that after the village church was consecrated, the first wedding to be held there was for a Druze couple. You just can't understand the secret of a place like Sarmada and its special harmony unless you've lived there or in one of the other small towns in Syria. I mean, there was even a very brave Christian among the leaders of the Great Syrian Revolt. The colonial-minded French who'd tried to divide the country up into petty states and factions could never understand why Christian freedom-fighters or revolutionaries would rebel against them; they simply denounced the whole lot of them as traitors. Or how when they threatened to confiscate the secret Druze Epistles of Wisdom, the people simply hid them with Muslim and Christian families for safekeeping.

Father Elias had grown old quickly, for sure. I hadn't seen

him in years but that captivating benevolence still shone in his smiling eyes. When I asked him if he remembered Hela Mansour's murder, he became downcast. 'Why do you want to go digging up the past?'

'I need to hear the whole story so I can find out exactly what happened. We might make a film about it...' I said.

'He that is without sin among you...' he repeated Christ's famous words a few times. Then he took a deep breath and let out a long sigh. 'You know, Rafi, the cruellest death is a death for honour's sake. Christ came and purified us of the sins of the body and the banal pleasures of the flesh, but you still see things like this happening. What happened to Hela Mansour, though, that was something else. It was the worst thing I've ever seen in my life.'

He looked distressed and started to take a few steps toward the rectory. 'I can still remember how the air smelt that night. The whole place reeked of death. The brothers had heard that she'd come back so me and a few others ran over to see them. At first, I figured it'd be better to take refuge in the church, to pray and spare myself the spectacle of a public death, but after I saw her with my own eyes, I felt I had to stop her brothers from behaving so stupidly. We went to their house – the one beside the flour mill – and we found Nawwaf, the eldest brother, there all by himself. He just stared at us indifferently until his other brothers all came running in and crowding around us. They were all on edge and smoking frantically. After they'd all arrived, one of them said, "She's back."

'"Where is she?" asked Nawwaf.

'"She's at the house," answered the youngest brother and then in the blink of an eye they scattered – as if they'd practised the ritual a thousand times before – and rooted out their rustiest weapons: razors, knives and cleavers. They started scraping off the rust and sharpening the blades as we begged them to see reason and to let her go in peace. We said we'd find a way to get her to leave Sarmada, but Nawwaf just loaded his shotgun and shot a few rounds into the air.

'He blew up, screaming at us, "Whoever feels like getting buried today, better just stay right there for one more minute!" He was deadly serious, you could see he was in torment and there was no way to soften his heart. We were terrified ourselves, so we turned to leave. He called after us, in a strangled voice, "Look, listen here!" When we turned back to look at him, he said …' Father Elias stopped to take a sip of the bitter tea. The generally forthright features of his face were roiled as he told me the story of that day, that he'd long since buried in the depths of his heart. 'He said, "Anyone who tries to protect her is going to give his mother a reason to grieve today. Just stay out of it." He fired a couple of more bullets into the air to emphasise his point.

'I prayed to Our Lady. And all of Sarmada prayed for Hela and her brothers. That was the most we could do … I guess, maybe we could've done something, but there was no one who felt they could do anything at the time.'

After he'd regained some of his customary good humour, I left Father Elias, promising I'd come back to see him and the others, whom I thought of as my family, very soon. As I walked away, I asked myself: Is anything clearer now? Does there even have to be a story here at all? And yet, I'd come across something enticing, even seductive, in the way the villagers told their stories, in that melange of confession, atonement and senseless chatter. I headed over to the oldest shop in the village, where people gathered to exchange the latest news and gossip. Mamdouh, the shopkeeper, welcomed me warmly just as he'd always done every time I returned and we sat down together on the bench in front of the shop. I asked him about Hela's brothers.

'What do you want to know about them for?'

'No reason in particular,' I said. 'I'm just curious. What happened to them? Who were they? Anything really.'

He poured the coffee and began: 'I was just a young boy back then, you know, about seven or eight years old. I can remember they used to come to the shop when my father was alive. I was terrified by the look of them, but my father – God rest his soul – always treated them very kindly. I asked him about them once and all he said was, "Son, there's nothing more precious in life than your honour and your good name. God help them."

'They'd come to the shop and give a one-word greeting, if that. Sometimes they wouldn't say anything at all, or they wouldn't return our greeting. They bought what they needed, usually paying in eggs or milk. Some of them would just up and disappear for a while; they were off trying to track her down. They even used to pay a reward to anyone who brought them information about her whereabouts. I saw them once, just in front of the shop here where we're sitting, they gave some Bedouin 100 lire to go looking for her.'

Salama came over, carrying his rusty shovel; I hardly ever saw him without it. He joined us at the front of the shop and, as usual, made a few sarcastic comments and took up the story where Mamdouh had left off. He explained that it was all Sarmada's fault. That all the villagers were to blame for what'd happened in one way or another. 'For a whole year after she ran off with that stranger, no one dared talk about it or take pleasure at the brothers' bad luck. And then, slowly with time, no one felt bad for them anymore. People started to say that it was their own damn fault.

A group of us went to see them: the Druze Initiates from the mountains, the village shaykhs, Father Elias, the archbishop; we all went over to talk to them. We tried to get them to move on with their lives. We told them that none of us were questioning their manhood. All those men of the cloth, all those local dignitaries reeled off parables and words of wisdom about God's will and submitting to fate and begged the brothers to forget about their sister. They told them that all they had to do was disown her and that her Creator would judge her for what she'd done. Everything's part of God's plan, they said, you've got to accept it. Nawwaf the eldest brother wasn't going to hear it, he was stubborn.'

Salama said he could still remember exactly what Nawwaf had

said to one of the shaykhs who told him to be reasonable, to have some perspective and obey God's will: 'This has nothing to do with God, Shaykh,' he answered softly. 'It's a lot bigger than God.' Old man Salama was all worked up and he was making wild circles in the air with his shovel: 'Well naturally the shaykhs and the other village elders weren't going to sit there and listen to all that blasphemy, so they just up and left, and let the brothers find their own way out of the wilderness of heartache back to right and reason. Not long afterwards, the brothers abandoned their family house in the centre of the village and moved out next to Majlis Hamza to get away from everyone else.'

I asked the other people at the shop about Azaday, the guy who'd stolen Hela away. Some of them had nothing but contempt for him, but a few others talked about him more ambiguously, more deferentially. As more and more people came to the shop, the conversation expanded to include other versions of the stories with everyone pitching in with his or her individual contribution. Some people remembered the story as their families had passed it down, while others had lived through the events themselves. A few had heard about what the couple had done and were full of respect for their courage. At that point, Shaykh Shaheen, the village elder, spoke up: 'Murder is a sin. You know, by running off and marrying someone outside the faith, she was really just returning to her origins.'

'What do you mean?' We asked. The Shaykh had to choose his words carefully: he wasn't allowed to reveal to us, the Uninitiated – we who'd not yet received the secrets of our faith – any specifics about the sect's esoteric wisdom. You see, Druze society is divided theologically into the Initiated, who strive to learn the Truth and apply it in their daily lives, and the Uninitiated, who don't have the right to read the Holy Texts and the commentaries written on them.

'The Druze call to faith was first made back in 408 AH, you know, 1018 AD,' said the Shaykh. 'It was announced to all the different denominations, sects, and religious communities in Fatimid Egypt and it spread into the Levant and the Taim Valley in particular. The creed was first set down by Hamza ibn Ali al-Zuzani, causing a schism with the Ismaili Shiites, whom they called "The belated Shaykhs". It was the first time in the history of Islam that polygamy was forbidden. Then the call to faith was completed in 436 AH. Anyone who joined the faith afterwards had to write out a formal declaration and swear that they held no remaining affiliations to any other sect or religion, and that they would never again hold such affiliations until the end of time, not even when their souls underwent periods of transmigration, which we call "Episodes of Revelation". Since at the time, a number of perfidious souls hid among the new Druze and pledged their faith, in every life, and in every generation, a number of non-Druze souls must be culled. These people leave the community of the faithful. They return to their origins, marrying outside the faith, and therefore, killing a woman who leaves the faith is obviously a sin; on the contrary, we should welcome it. It's simply a kind of automatic cleansing of the community, a purification of our blood and minds.' His view was supported by the Holy Epistles of Wisdom, which gave a religious justification for the act of leaving the custody of the closed community. It absolved the runaway for turning her back on the faith without any need for bloodshed.

'Well, then, why didn't the Mansour brothers accept it?' I asked the Shaykh.

'It was all about tradition,' he replied. 'Custom. To those who can't comprehend – or even appreciate – reason, it can seem more important than religion itself sometimes.'

'Do the Epistles of Wisdom say anything about whether killing is ever justified?' I asked.

The Shaykh was resolute in his wisdom. 'One isn't even allowed to strike or rebuke. This, too, is immoral and will not be tolerated. For us Druze, with our special understanding of God's oneness, all men and women are equal. Men aren't women's keepers. A man isn't allowed to have more than one wife, and women have the same rights in inheritance as men, or as specified in the will of the deceased. A Druze woman enjoys the same freedoms and is bound by the same obligations as a Druze man. Moreover, men aren't allowed to divorce their wives, or even threaten to. If he does, he can never take her back; it's unforgivable to even say the word. And this is intended to make divorce as difficult as possible.'

As I was saying goodbye to the people at the shop, Raifeh Umm Ibrahim came up to me and whispered, 'I was a friend of Hela's. She told me all her secrets. I even went with her a few times when she went to see him. He was such a stunning boy, just gorgeous. Nobody could resist him.' I walked with Raifeh as far as Poppy Bridge and along the way she painted a picture of the boy who'd snatched Hela away. 'He was so kind. His secret, his magic, was that he was a stranger. Strangers are always desirable, and Hela wasn't the only girl who was in love with him. He cast a spell on every girl in Sarmada. He was like a window onto a different world, colourful and exciting, not boring like this place here.'

Scraps of the picture began to come together as the scene formed mosaic-like before my eyes. I knew I was getting closer to Hela Mansour. At last, I'd arrived at something that resembled – if only superficially – the story Azza Tawfiq had told me. Yet it was still disconcerting: these kinds of stories were always travelling from person to person, being taken up – in a way, transmigrating. There was nothing to do but dig deeper, to extract more from more people, to jog memories to see what people had lived through at the time, to find out what they remembered about Azaday, and what happened to him.

The Sarmadans all said he was a wanderer from North Africa, one of those folks who went from village to village selling combs, lucky charms and candied flattery, carrying around ancient maps to look for clues in their search for hidden treasures. He arrived in Sarmada and set up camp. There he polished brass, repaired pots and pans, and decorated amulets with the magic ink he'd

inherited from his soothsaying ancestors in the Aurès Mountains. People said he could interpret the secret code of Dahiya bint
Lahiya, the seer of al-Bata al-Zanatiya, the greatest of the Amazigh
tribes. Now, of course, the seer initially won her fame by resisting the armies of the Muslim conquerors to avenge the murder
of her lover, Kusayla ibn Lamzam, but she remained a symbol of
the Amazigh spirit throughout the early periods of Islamic rule
in North Africa. Legend ascribed to her all manner of fantasy
and mystery and she became the authority upon whom everyone,
who chose to spend their lives among the occult sigils that could
unlock the talismans of life, relied.

Azaday was a member of the Lamzam family and could trace
his lineage all the way back to that Amazigh general himself,
the man who'd died defending the Aurès back before Islam had
extended its rule over the whole of North Africa. And yet, beneath
the ashes, the Amazigh character remained. Azaday, who'd been
brought up in the circus of the Aurèsian landscape, cut a striking figure in small-town Sarmada. He could move a broom with
his eyes and take a sand grouse, flying along in a migrating flock,
and bring it crashing down to the ground in front of his audience.
He had a strangely shaped wooden guitar that he played, which
made Daham, the leper's dog, howl all night long, even though it'd
been dumb for years. Once he was done amazing Sarmada with
his marvels, he'd sit down and sing to them with his enchanting
voice. They were crazy about his songs, which remained in their
heads for weeks on end. He even won the respect and approval
of the five brothers, who were charmed by his many talents. The
middle brother even went so far as to invite him over.

They stayed up all night, getting drunk with the help of a bottle
of matured arak. Hela came in, carrying a huge tray bedecked
with all manner of mezze. She sat opposite Azaday, the Algerian
come to the East – although they simply called all North Africans
'Moroccans' – and examined him silently. Her gaze was all curiosity; it was her love of discovery, her heart laid bare. Something

about him caused her to forget all the advice Druze girls were given: beware strangers for there's no happily-ever-after for Druze who stray outside the narrow confines of the sect.

He was thirty-one and copiously – arrestingly – masculine. After a second glass of arak, he started to sing a strange ballad called *Aynuva and Ghariba*. The vast hollow of the house filled with his mesmerising voice. Mysterious Amazigh words that carried the mountain air of the Aurès, and which none of them could understand – apart from 'Forest beast' and 'O Father! O Father!' – faded into nothingness. They asked him to explain the lyrics, so he did his best to find Arabic equivalents.

O Father, open the door!
Daughter, silence your bracelets' clanging.
O Father, I fear the forest beast!
Me too, dear daughter, me too.

His songs transformed the house into a trap of gentle affection. Hela was being worn down, and as she sat there across from the door, her heart opened up wider and wider; the bolts of good counsel be damned. The song carried her off to another clime and when he turned to look at her, a secret thread began to stitch her destiny to that of this vagabond Berber. He could feel her stare swirling around him and he knew that his extraordinary journey – from the Algerian mountains in remotest North Africa to Sarmada – had all been for this: to delight in that gaze as it set his heart alight. He'd promised himself that he'd be nothing but a neutral observer, only an itinerant earning his daily bread and seeking out his roots here in the Levant; she made him want to go back on his word.

༄

A band of young Africans were playing music in front of the statue of Saint Michel and people had gathered around to listen.

Nonetheless, neither the sound of banging drums and clattering shakers, nor an African voice filling the air could keep me from listening closely as the physics professor continued her tale. I was beginning to doubt whether folk memory alone could have produced all those astonishing details, preserved all those expressive images and reflections from one generation to the next. She'd buried the little cowbell, her will, and her mother's bracelets beneath the mulberry tree and walked out of the house to face them. She continued, recounting all that her memory granted from beyond the grave.

They'd run away to Damascus and got married there. They took fake names because they were being hunted by a team of dogged trackers, but it was difficult to disguise their true identities as they'd failed to cross the border and get decoy papers printed. Because of her father's legacy as a hero of the Great Revolt, all those with higher authority in the mountains spread the word at the border passes that Azaday was a dangerous criminal who was wanted by the security forces, and so they were harassed everywhere they went. They became a couple of easy targets, who were ever vulnerable to blackmail and the threat of exposure. It wasn't very hard to figure out who they were, what with his Algerian accent, and it made it all but impossible for them to hide out.

There was nothing left for them to do but to take refuge with the Shammar tribe of Bedouins for a while. Azaday spent years trying to get them into Iraq and Turkey to no avail and twice they fell into the hands of Camel Corps soldiers, whom her brothers had bribed. They never stayed in one place for more than a week and constantly being on the run had ground them all the way down by the time they reached Zabadani. They remained there for a week with the smugglers and then Azaday daringly crossed the border into Lebanon alone and back to make sure it was safe. He returned ecstatic and hopeful: they'd cross the border with the smugglers. He'd tested the route himself and confirmed that nothing could go wrong. Promise shone once again in the distance and announced an end to their days of banishment. They would get as far away as they could, and go back to Algeria. Dreams surged out before her. Hela smiled, but there was some sadness in her eyes. She'd placed a bet on time; she'd sought news of her brothers from the itinerant peddlers and coppersmiths who passed through Sarmada, and yet now she couldn't deny feeling the astonishing relief of a death forestalled. She'd heard about what had happened to them, how they'd abnegated and consecrated, and now it was time to decide: vanish or go back?

Azza Tawfiq laid out in detail the events of that night. Azaday was thunderstruck when Hela told him she'd had enough and had decided to go back. 'I can still hear his voice, the echo of his words, how he begged me to stay, not to be stupid and go back. He started cursing in Amazigh and pleading with me in my mountain Arabic. He tried everything he could to get me to change my mind: charms, begging, threats and promises. I answered every attempt with a single refrain, uttered calmly but firmly, "I have to go back." He lost it. He started beating his head against the wall. He tore at his clothes. He threw himself at my feet.

'"I have to go back …"

'He grabbed me by the shoulders and shook me. He squeezed my hands, his nails dug into my skin.

'"I have to go back …"

'I just couldn't explain to him that I'd made my decision for the good of us all. I wanted to give him the chance to have a life free of fear. We'd been moving from town to town for months on end. We'd tried our luck in every inch of Syria, from the north to the south, from the coast to the desert, scrambling like stalked prey. The mere hint that someone else nearby was from the mountains made us run off in a panic. My brothers' plight had won the sympathy of everyone in the Druze mountains and the news that they'd isolated themselves from the rest of society had spread beyond the region and won them pity beyond the sect. Not a single person who heard the story forgave me for what I'd done.

I'd been sentenced to death for the lives of five of Sarmada's best. We were cursed. There was nowhere left for us to go, not in Syria, maybe not even in the whole world.

'I knew how stubborn my brothers could be. They'd inherited that bloody-mindedness from our forefathers, that severity; it was like a masochistic ritual with them. It was like I was committing murder a thousand times a day. There was nothing I could do except go back and let them live again. I held him that night. It was an agony I'd only ever felt twice in my life: the day my mother died and the day Princess was put down. For a moment, I felt that perhaps we could make it to Beirut and from there to somewhere safe and that I could be as happy as the rest of God's creation, but I just didn't want to go on anymore.'

At dawn, she slipped out of the rented house in Zabadani without waking him and went to Damascus. There, she caught a bus from the Bab al-Musalla station and reached Sarmada on Tuesday evening after a light rain. She walked to her old house to pray that God would be merciful to her mother, and to commemorate her old life, to ask the old place to forgive her, and to bury her will. She then continued down the paths that ran alongside Princess' cliff to face them in the square like a lamb to the slaughter. She'd left him behind; the man who'd been so good at inventing stories, at dazzling even the most frigid hearts, and a dozen things besides. The man who aroused wonder wherever he went, who sold potions and handkerchiefs perfumed with good fortune, who played that strange guitar of his and sang songs, which he made up on the spot, in that enchanting voice, who interpreted dreams. He was sound asleep when she left him. He'd finally got her to promise that she'd go to Beirut with him in a couple of days. She knew it was a lie when she said it.'

Azza Tawfiq stopped speaking. Her mood changed and she asked me for a cigarette. She lit it and her gaze drifted, not off into the distance, but deep inside. Her left foot bobbed constantly as she spoke as if she were casting off a long-kept silence, as if she were finally shedding a heavy burden after endless toil. I had nothing I wanted to say. She looked out absent-mindedly toward the Seine. You could see the Louvre in the distance and the Latin Quarter was buzzing with life. She began to stroke her left palm. There was a small wart and dark spots where two warts used to be. She noticed I was looking at her palm, but she didn't hide it. She simply whispered, sardonically, 'I never could get rid of these warts. For that you need a psychologist. The only way to get rid of them is the power of suggestion. One difference between Hela and me is that she managed to do it by using an old Aramaic cure. But me in Paris in 2010, I've had three laser procedures for them and they're still not fully cured. Maybe I need to go back to Sarmada, to the Salt Spring, to cure them.' Azza looked me straight in the eye. 'You know the Salt Spring, of course?'

'Yes, I remember it. We used to go there when I was little to drink the cold water. We'd walk down four stone steps and scoop the water up. It tastes better than Evian if you ask me.' That was my attempt at lightening the mood, but she didn't flinch. There was only a wan smile sketched on her lips. She went on, confident and unwavering; she wanted me to know every last detail, to convince me it was true, and to free herself. So she told me how she walked out of the old house and toward the square to greet her fate.

'I was rubbing my hand as I walked towards them, remember-ing the Salt Spring and my cow, Princess. I'd cured my warts with Aunt Rosa's remedy on the same day Princess fell from the cliff … I was there the day she fell down off the cliff. I was only about eight years old and I was following the old Aramaic cure that Aunt Rosa, the old Christian medicine woman, had given me along with two lumps of rock salt. "Don't speak to anyone," she said. "Don't look behind you. And don't return anyone's greeting. Just go to the spring and throw the salt in, and then come back the same way you went."

'I went to the Salt Spring, performed the rite, and repeated three times: "My warts, O Spring, dissolve, as salt dissolves in water!" I went home and fell asleep in my mother's arms. I woke with a start: outside there was a commotion. I got up to see what was going on. My father and two other men were sharpening butcher knives and then they hurried off. I followed them to the cave in the valley below the cliff where people used to take shelter from French air raids. The village thoroughfare ran alongside the cliff that overhung the cave and there was a sliver of rock that jutted out and led to a dead end.

'I saw all the villagers heading for the bottom of the cliff, staring up at the huge cow as it mooed plaintively for help. I can still remember the look in her eye: a faint glimmer of hope that they might save her from her fatal predicament.'

♨

Old man Salama was one of the ones who'd been getting ready in case Princess should fall. He said he could remember it as if it were yesterday: Princess was the most famous cow in the whole area. No one could quite understand how exactly she'd managed to set the terms, how she'd won them all over, silenced their mocking, and maintained her poise until they finally realised that she was something special. They ended up giving her a name that matched her imperious bearing, breaking the long-standing tradition that only thoroughbred Arabian horses merited such names.

'Princess never wore a halter so she'd nearly trample the village cowhands when they came to take her to pasture. She once went two days without any water because she refused to drink with the other cows in the herd and when they tried to stall her with another cow, she knocked down a pair of wooden doors and slammed her stubborn head against the wall. Her milk was the best though, the most abundant and delicious in the whole region.'

Salama went on, reviving the memories of his peers gathered there in front of Mamdouh's shop: 'One time she was in heat and the village bull couldn't mount her, so she had to spend a whole week in heat until we brought her a proper stud bull from the north. After hours of resisting and butting, he finally mounted her. She got that prize bull in the neck with her horn, but at long last she let out a moan of pleasure that rang through the village. Women came ululating and we danced the Dabke until the morning. It was the first time we'd ever put on a wedding for someone that wasn't human.' He laughed, as did everyone else.

'Well then how come this super-cow suffered such a shabby death?' I asked them, hoping to compare the memories of the villagers to what Azza Tawfiq had told me in Paris.

'The cow went after strange whims,' Salama said. 'She wandered off, following the green grass that took her from the safety of the familiar to the lure of the unknown. She walked along the edge of the cliff, looking for the freshest, virgin shoots. She drifted off away from her natural route in search of sweet mallow and tempting clover.'

Salama stopped and pointed to the nearby cliff. He turned to me. 'See there? Every day she went down that path towards the Salt Spring to drink. Except that day, she stopped unexpectedly near where the cliff hangs over the cave; she'd spotted a little path that took her right up over the roof of the cave. To her right there was a massive drop and to her left a wall of basalt. The path was narrow and it ended at a boulder that blocked the way forward. It was barely wide enough for her; she couldn't go back, she couldn't go forward, and of course she couldn't turn around and head out front-first.

She ate her fill and then when she realised she was stuck, she mooed a few times. A crowd gathered and we tried everything to save her from what seemed like certain death. We tried to use strong ropes, but the climbers couldn't get to her to wrap the ropes around her body. We went around to all the houses in the village and got all the foam mattresses out of the parlours and the women collected tattered clothes and stuffed sacks with straw. Hamoud supervised the creation of a safety net made out of blankets, mattresses, rugs and yarn. In the heat of the moment, he even tore off his carefully pressed coat and threw it on top of the surreal textile pile. I bet that was the strangest safety net ever made. But, you see, the problem was that it wouldn't have saved a mountain goat let alone a cow as big as Princess! The ground wasn't level and the whole idea was just a bit silly. People can get somewhat foolish and childlike when they're desperate.

'After four hours we still didn't have anything to show for all our effort. All we could do was pray for a miracle – maybe the cow would sprout wings. When our imagination had gone as far as that, we knew it was time to start getting out the knives and cleavers. We spread out along the bottom of the cliff and started sharpening, just waiting for her to fall!'

I left Salama at the shop with the other men and walked over to the cliff. The place hadn't changed in all that time. It was the setting of my childhood, too, but I don't want to force my memories into the story just yet. I thought back on my life and work, about constantly being swamped making those films about Bridging East and West, those interminable months of research and discussion – everything had to be just right so the camera could make concrete images out of my paper ideas – and then I met Azza Tawfiq in Paris. She not only upended my schedule, but – as I'd later discover – she was also the spark that set my whole life up in flames.

I looked up at Princess' cliff, half-expecting Hela Mansour to walk past. It was as if time were commixed. A place can't be an anchored moment. All it takes is a little memory and some storytelling, and then time begins to flow. It was my job to set the scene, just as Azza Tawfiq had seen it in her previous life, just how she'd told it to me, and also how the people of Sarmada were recounting the story, here and now. Once I'd added some of my own perspective and imagination, it went like this:

Three knives, two daggers and a cleaver waiting below as the body fell through the air to the ringing of the bell around her neck.

The blades plunged into the carcass from every side. They cut off her limbs, and blood gushed over their faces and clothing. Her final groan terrified the crowd but as it faded away, the precious cow fell silent. The crowd jumped back to avoid the spurting blood and its sticky splatter, expanding the circle of spectators that had grown tighter and tighter around the stiff, heaped carcass lying on the rocky ground. One of the most skilful butchers there was put in charge of beheading the creature. One carefully gauged blow of the cleaver and the little bell fell from its neck and rolled down to the foot of the cliff. Hela Mansour's youngest brother went after it and brought it home to her as a token of the day.

The tale of Princess' demise was over, I felt. Now it was time to head over to the Salt Spring and circle around the cliff, waiting for her to arrive at the mercy of this summer heat that simply wouldn't let up. I stopped to examine the craggy cliff face and to look down the path all the way to the end, where Hela Mansour was slaughtered. I spent a long time just looking in the midst of what seemed like a thicket of oppressive calm. Steam rose up from the asphalt as if it were about to melt and the air was heavy with an alien heat. My body felt weighed down suddenly, and then instantly lighter. I trembled and broke out in a cold sweat. Something like a light drizzle fell on my face. Hela's Mansour's body had settled, it seemed, inside my own. We'd melded and she now occupied my body. I didn't realise it, but suddenly I was walking along beside her, or through her. I'd become her, she'd become me, and together we returned to that Tuesday evening in 1968.

She spotted her brothers coming toward her in the distance – a gang of bearded men clearly carrying knives and cleavers like the ones she'd seen thirteen years before, on the day Princess fell from the cliff.

She closed her dark eyes – just as she'd done when she watched that scene with her brothers all those years ago – and arrived on the stage for a scene she'd never imagined would be replayed on her own body as the price for her deadly defection with an outsider. They slowed down and eventually stopped, standing in a semicircle. I stepped forward into the centre. Their beards masked their faces, but she knew each one by the look of his eyes. She wished she could throw her arms around them, embrace them one by one, and say, 'I'm tired of running,' but she didn't. She just listened to the eerie silence, which was broken only by the cold whistling wind coming down from the North. One brother's eyes articulated sorrow and longing as if to say 'I missed you,' but his voice, sad and cracking, said only, 'Why'd you do it?' and seized up.

Rain didn't fall although the sky darkened with clouds. Nawwaf came up to us – to me who'd become her – roaring and snarling, and plunged his knife through her scarlet shirt into her chest as it continued to rise and fall rapidly. A shivering spasm came over her whole body as she sank to the ground. Together we watched the heavy clouds break and become snowflakes. I could feel the blade burying itself in my chest as I watched. As she fell to the ground, she looked up to the sky above and summoned up all her remaining strength. 'Are you satisfied now? Anything else you want from me, God?' she cried, her voice passing through the cloying blood that tasted salty in her throat.

I screamed alongside her, 'Anything else you want from me, God?' Her memories began appearing before her eyes in an uncanny flow as her numb body longed only to fall and rest. And yet the lightness gave her the feeling of flying. I watched the tape of her life streaming before me: school papers, old friends, her brothers carrying her around, laughing at her mischief, passing her from shoulder to shoulder, her father's kindly eyes, her mother's divine laugh, the mulberry tree at her old house, berries sweet like nectar.

He withdrew his knife and took a step back, permitting the others to come forward and stab her in the neck, the back and torso. She glimpsed the Salt Spring as she fell. The swift current of her memory whirled. Milk thistle didn't help with the warts. The old medicine woman. The church bells she loved so much. The muezzin calling morning prayer. Druze shaykhs reciting the Epistles of Wisdom or the story of Judgment Day on the last evening of the Feast of Sacrifice. The scent of lit candles in the majlis. Milk sloshing melodiously in stomach bags. Women lamenting a death.

The fourth knife pierced her windpipe just below the neck. She tasted only salt; her body grew torpid; her head teemed with memories. Gushing blood stained her mind.

The smell of roses on the morning of Holy Wednesday. Running to pick the supplest red poppy anemones, oleander, daisies, sweet clover, pennyroyal and rosemary, which she soaked in an earthenware pot and left out under the stars of the spring night sky. In the morning on the second Wednesday in April, she'd wash her body with the flower infusion, as was the ritual, to be protected from snakes and scorpions for an entire year. Old tales. Weddings and pranks. Amulets and strings that could change one's destiny. My warts, O Spring, dissolve!

Her belly was rent open from one hip to the other. She fell to the ground and thrust her hands into the muddy dirt that was mixed with her own warm blood. My warts, O Spring, dissolve. Her mind was clear but for a gentle peal that withered into a still whiteness.

At that point, I left her to collapse, dead, and came out of her; or she came out of me – I don't know which. But I watched the final scene, standing there by the cliff, soaked with sweat, searching my soul. There was a gluey taste in my mouth, acrid like blood. One of them stepped forward and drove his knee into her back. He pulled her head back by the hair. With a twitch of her neck and a swift movement, her head was severed. They took out their razors, smeared their faces with her blood, and began to shave their beards off in clumps that fell onto her corpse. They didn't say a word. They stood and took in the scene as a light drizzle of rain began to fall, and an unfamiliar numbness pricked their faces. A great burden had been lifted, but it was as if it'd flowed out with the blood and settled somewhere in their chests; the burden was a voice they didn't want to hear. They squeezed their eyes shut to hold back the tears that burst out despite them when the wind blew away the tufts of hair covering her body. They retreated hastily and were met with cheering women ululating and men standing dry-eyed as rain fell from the gloomy sky.

The taste of blood in my mouth was real. I fainted. The neighbours carried me over to their house where I was given a glass of cold water and began to regain some of my strength. Friends and relatives came running, 'What's wrong? Is everything okay?'

'Nothing to worry about,' answered the man of the house. 'It's just a touch of sun.'

ﻉﻼ

Panning the video camera, I captured the whole of Sarmada from the top of the hill – a panorama of the quiet little village. When I got down from the hill, I filmed the paths, focused on the old stone houses, the cliff, the Mansour family's detached homestead by the old mill, Cannon Hill – it got that name because it was where the French had set up their cannon when they were shelling the town and its environs. I filmed the rest of the valley, Farida's shed, the terebinth tree, the myrtle, Wool Creek, until I got to the Mansour family's old house. The aged smell of the place enveloped me as I kicked open the old gate, which hadn't been replaced in decades. It opened with a screech. The dotty old mulberry tree stood in the centre of the garden. It made me feel like we'd known each other for years. I filmed everything I could and then sat down to contemplate the ruination. It occurred to me to search through the soil under the mulberry tree so I started to dig. My hands were no use so I went round to Salama's house to borrow a shovel.

I got down to work. I dug up the earth around the trunk down to an arm's length, but found no sign of the will, or the bracelets, or the bell. I suddenly realised I was being ridiculous and stopped.

Salama, with his narrow brown eyes and wrinkled face, came over to see what I was up to and asked me what I was looking for. 'Nothing … It was just a stupid idea I had.'

'You're not the first person to go looking for treasure under there,' he said. 'We've dug down under the ruins of this house two or three times already and we didn't find anything except for an old copper cowbell.' I was dumbstruck. 'The bell's round the neck of one of the cowhand's cows now.'

'Really?'

'Follow me.' He led me to Poppy Bridge. A man was leading a herd of nineteen cows back from the poppy fields. The herd walked calmly past us; each cow had a copper bell around its neck. Salama went up to one of them and snatched off its bell. It was about as big as a fist and slightly dented. He held it out to me and said, 'I found this buried in the Mansours' garden.' I started laughing, imagining how the physics professor would react when I handed her the bell. It didn't prove anything, not that transmigration was real or that reality had transmigrated. Anyone could be Hela Mansour or not. And yet, had she not come over me? I'd taken the stabs alongside her. I'd choked on the sour blood in her throat. I watched her memories soar and touched the awesome darkness as she lay there, motionless.

I left her body, or she left mine. And then the place I'd fled from opened up before me: Sarmada. I hadn't realised that Sarmada was a part of me, and that I was a part of it. But now I could see – without eyes – and hear the rush of people's stories and dreams; the simple setting teemed. I wasn't the same 'me' anymore. I wasn't dying to get away as I usually was during my visits. I wasn't oppressed by the customary, crushing boredom. The dull sluggishness of life here didn't remind me of the brisk city rhythms of my beloved Dubai, Paris, Amsterdam and London. I craved Sarmada all of a sudden, preferred it, and for the first time, I realised that I'd merely been searching for something within myself the farther afield I went and that I could only find it here.

I ambled over to my old house and went in. With new eyes, I discovered mulberries, pomegranates, prickly pears, a chicken coop, and a pen for sheep and goats in our garden. Versions of me appeared: the baby, the child, the teenager. I watched time flow. Who had I been? How come I hadn't known him before? I'd spent all that time struggling to change who I was, to run away from myself; masquerading in a different language, a different guise, to be accepted by another place, another time. I examined the small, dented bell, ignoring a torrent of phone calls. I began to discern my inner self, to see that I'd been wearing deformed masks for all those years as they now began to fall away. Time, it seemed, had passed over our house; it had passed over Sarmada entirely. Things had only got smaller, and worn out.

I went up to the second floor, my favourite room upstairs in my grandfather's house; it was my childhood stamping ground. The plains of the Hauran ran down to the horizon, bordered by a vast and rocky stretch of basalt that continued deep into the heart of the Lajat. Old sounds, images and smells came toddling forward and a loss-laden epiphany throbbed within me. A voice came over the village loud speaker: 'We regret to announce the passing of Farida bint Fadda. May God show her mercy and comfort those she leaves behind.'

The town broke out in whispers: how crass! Whoever decided to broadcast the news of Farida's death had clearly intended to ridicule her passing. The sounds of mourning wrenched me away from Hela Mansour, Azza Tawfiq, and my momentary fancy of sinking into memory, and returned me to reality. I realised – with a start – that it had been a week and I still hadn't told anyone in Dubai what I was up to. I'd come under the pretext of work and was actually meant to be in Damascus, not here. Reality's tenacious logic set me back on track: I called my boss and told him there'd been a death in the family. I asked for a week off, promising to make up the time I missed, and he grudgingly gave in. I answered a text from the physics professor, who said she wished she could be there with me and see what I was seeing. I told her I'd bring her a Sarmadan surprise and turned off my mobile.

I walked downstairs and joined a group hurrying over to Farida's place. I asked why they'd cheapened her death by announcing it like that, but the only person who'd answer me was Salama. 'Farida was free-spirited,' he said. 'She opened her door to every young man in the village. She slept with any man she felt like. God have mercy on her. Her secret's with the Lord and she's his problem now.'

'What do you mean "She opened her door to every man in the village?"'

'She was a whore, son!' he barked at me. 'Don't you get it?' He stormed off, muttering to himself and leaning on his battered old shovel.

People were getting louder and louder until they were almost shouting. The village, normally oppressed with silence, was rife with tension. I walked toward the uproar. A group of men were carrying the corpse and improvising a slapdash funeral service; the shaykhs had refused to pray over the body. She was buried that evening far outside the town limits. Other people, meanwhile, rummaged through all her possessions. The time had come to settle the score for her liberal youth. It was like a group assassination of someone who'd tried to break through the strictures of all that was accepted and approved.

I simply couldn't understand why no one had said anything about Farida while she was still alive. Why hadn't they put her on trial or killed her even? They'd all consented to Hela Mansour's murder after all; they'd stood by and done nothing. How exactly does memory get passed on from one generation to the next? How does it pass down the stories of scandal, of those who've violated the tyranny of hidebound sectarian and tribal law? How could the people have tolerated a woman who'd corrupted all the young men in Sarmada year after year? She'd allowed them to express their manhood directly through her body rather than through masturbation, or having sex with farm animals, or exploring male bodies and discovering the anal and phallic thrills of gay sex. Classic Freudian questions, but in a place so secretive and so harsh, the ready-made answers can't help but seem so silly. If Farida had lived in the West, she'd have been prosecuted, and maybe even locked away for life as a child molester. True, they weren't exactly children, although they were under eighteen, but some people got married as young as fifteen in the village. A whole generation of men in Sarmada crossed into manhood over her body's bridge. But in the East – and maybe specifically in Sarmada – what she'd done was more like saint's work, and the trial only took place now that she was dead.

Let's put moral judgments aside for a moment and tell the tale from the very start. Let's try to put the story back together and maybe Sarmada will give me a few more clues to help me try to understand how I fit in with these people who made me who I am, who imprinted their rashness on me, who nursed me – though I don't know from where – with the waters of rage, fear, joy and gloom.

Farida struck my thoughts like a bolt of lightning, driving out Azza Tawfiq, Hela Mansour, and everything else that had happened, or at least setting them aside for later. I was pelted by the memories swirling around me and by the memory of that delightful day. Farida appeared to me, as I tried to remember her, the way she looked when I was ten years old.

I had an aunt who was the most famous seamstress in the whole region. She used to receive her customers in her bedroom, which she'd made into a workshop, and she used the south-facing room as a fitting room. I used to love that room and often slept there. I discovered that the women weren't embarrassed to change in front of me as I was so young, especially not when I pretended to be asleep. The ritual of covertly watching the women undress was my little secret. It was thrilling although I didn't yet know why.

Except Farida had figured me out; she knew I used to watch her undress. One day, she came in as I was pretending to be asleep, with the covers pulled over my head except for a tiny gap through which I could see her body. With her inimitable delicacy, she slowly stripped off and she squeezed her breasts together with a knowing smile. I felt a stab of pain as she undid her bra and let one of her pomegranate breasts spill out. It bobbed slightly and fell still. She tucked her breast back into her bra and began to take off her skirt in a kind of striptease. She pinched her skirt and slid it down to the floor, shimmying her hips, exposing her oaken torso, which rested on tender and bulging thighs of an intoxicatingly dark brown. Cognisant of the fact that she was being watched by a young voyeur, she twirled around completely, showing off her African-round bottom. Her underwear did nothing to conceal it, just divided it into two equal halves that each called out to me wildly. Her vulva nearly pushed through her shiny black panties; the top was rounded, but you could make out the beginning of her slit and at the sides there were a few red bumps from frequent shaving. The sight of her nakedness destroyed me. A hyena was whooping inside of me. I felt numbing pulses tickling my pelvis. And here was my first erection, come to herald the beginning of a tortuous relationship between me and that skinny body lying beneath the sheets, completely covered but for a tiny aperture on that hot summer day.

When she heard the deep, hot, reptilian panting I couldn't hold back, she grinned. She tried on the new dress and then quickly took it off. She put her own dress back on and on her way out, crept up to my lair and tore the covers off my sweaty face. She laughed loudly, causing my aunt in the next room to ask if everything was all right. She winked at me and smiled the sweetest sinful smile. 'What would you say if I told your aunt, you little runt?' And walked out. Those were the only words I ever heard her say.

Of course, I told my aunt about it and was immediately banished from that exquisite ambush. She screened off the fitting room and forbade me from ever going in there again. Farida remained a longed-for fantasy, which faded with time until I forgot all about it – only to remember it tonight. The only reason I'd been brought here was to bury Farida, I felt, or rather to revive her, to bring her back to life – for that alone. The professor's voice echoed in my mind, as she repeated Einstein's saying, reminding me to free myself, to open my memory and live life up to the very fullest: 'As far as the laws of mathematics refer to reality, they are not certain; as far as they are certain, they do not refer to reality.'

Chapter Two

Farida

Not two weeks after Hela Mansour returned to the village by the southern road to face her terrible fate, Farida arrived in a Land Rover. She was absolutely stunning: she had big, kohled eyes and long dark lashes, she was tall – taller than 5 foot 8 – and svelte, and she had a beguiling gait. If she'd been born nowadays, she'd have certainly become a model. This was the woman who would change the emotional texture of Sarmada for years to come, back before she was consumed by oblivion, before her life came to an end on this very evening.

I had to return. Sarmada had become Scheherazade, weaving the story of my home, so that I could come to realise, unsettlingly, that everything I'd ever done in my career had been nothing more than a reaction, a reflex without grounds. And grounds here means only one thing: belief. I saw Sarmada in a new light. Farida had thrown open the windows of my memory. A single sentence out of my childhood and a few dozen conversations stored away in the hearts and minds of the villagers, that was what I had to dredge up. As I rescued those memories from the darkness, Sarmada burst upon me in all its seductive charm, its force, its depth and its captivating plainness.

Sarmada had been through a bitter winter the year Farida came; and two years after the Six Day War, the country was still suffering from its defeat. A terrible emptiness had engulfed the village, its people, the trees and the stones, in a heavy silence. After Hela's murder, most people in Sarmada had an uncomfortable, choking feeling. The image of her being slaughtered had tainted the village mood; it became wearisome, and the air was heavy with guilt. Places, like people, live and feel: they hate, they love, and their moods deteriorate. They get bored, too. You can walk into any town or city in the world and figure out its mood before you've even drunk your first glass of the local water.

Salama explained to me what it was like. 'Like having a hairball stuck in your throat.' 'If it hadn't been for Farida, I don't think we'd have ever been happy again,' he added whispering. I asked people about Farida. I loitered around streets and hangouts. I met people, listened carefully, wrote and took notes – all acts of opportunism that weighed on my soul and made me think again and again about how blind I'd been. How had I overlooked all that was happening around me? Was it really true that all this life, all this coming and going, and the anger and uproar, had been here beside me the whole time? Was it true that the great questions and poignant answers had been with me for more than thirty years while I was busy chasing dreams in Paris and delusions in Dubai?

I looked anew at every proudly solid stone, at the trees and streams. I was amazed by the gutters coming down off the roofs, which were tiled with stone, cement and mud. I wandered through the desert of stories. I gathered everything up and saw that it made a banquet with enough for everyone: the banquet of life, most likely. But I'd better disappear and let the place tell its own story. I'll watch from a distance, silent but with every sense piqued. I won't interfere; I'll simply record it all and send it to the physics professor waiting for me in Paris.

The people of Sarmada were living with a shooting pain that seemed to burn at something inside of them. A kind of remorse had taken hold of many of those who'd witnessed Hela Mansour's

44

murder; it was a feeling that they, too, were butchers. Hela Mansour had taken away something they'd got used to. She'd refused to give them the dignity of a secret story to pass around behind her back, something to chew the fat over, to embellish or pare down as required, as they'd done over those many years since she'd run away with her Amazigh lover. No, instead, she'd proclaimed her return and lanced the boil herself. She'd decided for herself how it would end and surrendered to fate without reservation. They wanted a new story, something to wipe away the trace of that disgraceful death. Their life was as meaningless as it had ever been and the place simply couldn't take the guilt much longer.

It surely didn't help that they couldn't bring themselves to forgive the Mansour brothers for what they'd done. They tried the best they could, but they still harboured a vague disapproval. Quietly and deeply confused, the brothers withdrew, and over the next few years each would suffer his own individual collapse. The youngest emigrated to Colombia after experiencing the ecstasy of Farida's body and then being denied her love. Two of the brothers were drawn to Khalwat al-Bayada, the hermitage of ascetic Druze shaykhs in Lebanon, who – cut off from the world and worldly life for the rest of their lives – were free to unlock the secrets of the Epistles of Wisdom and write commentaries on The Unique Text, while they waited on the doorstep of God's house in case He should choose to purify their hearts. Five years later, the fourth brother was to die fighting in the October War, and Nawwaf was left alone. He returned to the house in the centre of the village and stood guard over the shadows. He spoke to the mulberry tree and at every full moon, he wept and, as if howling, repeated over and over, 'Forgive me, Hela, forgive me…'

The day Farida arrived in Sarmada with Salman al-Khattar, the driver and gambler, she was twenty-six. He brought her back in his famous car after he'd spent three nights in the eastern district. The man risked everything like someone who didn't care if he won or lost but played only for the thrill of the bet. It was a habit he'd learnt from life itself: nothing's worth holding onto. He spent money with a kind of lunatic generosity, living by the motto: Spend and ye shall receive! On that particular occasion, just as he was about to fold the rubbish hand he'd been dealt, he spotted that magnificent figure walk up, dazzling, the faint light falling over her as she crossed the courtyard of the mountain house. His mood did a complete one-eighty. Luck showered him with considerable winnings and, in fact, right at that moment it began planning a whole new destiny for him.

The card-sharps from the neighbouring village of al-Manabi had come together that night; they were known for their skill and for turning anything and everything into a bet. No matter what happened in the village, it was always met by the question 'Care to make things interesting?'

But he, Salman al-Khattar that is, had no trouble winning at sette e mezzo, poker, blackjack and baccarat. Not only the Queen of Hearts, but the Queen of Clubs was smiling at him. One unlikely hunch after another never betrayed him and the pile of cash and valuables in front of him got bigger and bigger.

Muaz, whose house they were playing at, bet everything he had: his wife's bracelets, the Rado Diastar watch he'd won off a guy in Beirut, and yet the guest kept on winning. Even when Salman got nervous and figured it'd be safer to lose a few hands, Lady Luck had other ideas; the pile of money, watches, gold necklaces and wives' bracelets only grew. The more he tried to lose, the more winnings came flowing in. In the end, the men of the house and the gamblers of al-Manabi lost everything. Salman packed all his winnings into a hessian sack and got ready to leave. He didn't want to patronise those hardened gamblers; after all, offering to give them back some of what he'd won would've been worse than winning it in the first place. He tried to stay calm and to hide his excitement; he'd never won so much in his entire life! And that was when Farida strolled up, bold as anything, electrifying the tension among them. As they tried to scrape up the shame of their losses, she baldly announced, 'The jackpot's still up for grabs.'

They looked up. She was all defiance, all insistence, and any standing they'd felt evaporated in an instant. 'One last hand,' she said to Salman. 'You win, you get to keep everything and you get to marry me. You lose, you give it all back ... but you still get me.' Her poor uncle didn't know what to think. His jaw dropped and all he could do was wait to hear an answer. Salman didn't need to be asked twice: those big, patently desiring eyes had stirred his heart and filled his mind with a sweet and sticky madness.

As chivalrous as any nobleman, he emptied his winnings out onto the table and said, 'I lose. Go get ready.' He threw the empty sack on the floor and turned to the others. 'Tell the Shaykh he's got a ceremony to perform.'

She drove away with him, leaving her cousins and relatives behind. They couldn't hide how happy they were that she'd saved them from the idiocy they'd brought on themselves; they'd almost been forced to unload a pistol clip into the lucky stranger's skull. Bitterly, but with grim smiles, they sat down to divide up what they'd wagered.

She arrived in Sarmada, stepping down from the Land Rover in her crimson dress, which, along with her timid gait, her giraffe-like neck, and her lovely, big eyes, stayed embedded in the memory of many. The first person to lay eyes on her was Aboud Scatterbrains. His jaw dropped and his eyes glazed over; her beauty – which would soon be the death of him – laid him out. A number of nosy people came to Salman al-Khattar's house to ask about this vision of loveliness who'd come out of nowhere. 'Who is she? What's she doing at the al-Khattar's?'

Salman's mother, Fadila, put an end to the questions: 'The wedding party's next Thursday. It'll go on for three nights.'

Sarmada danced until dawn. The village needed to forget the

bloodbath that had taken place two weeks before and the fear that had bound many in its chains. On foggy days, they could see Hela Mansour's headless ghost roaming through the village after midnight, trying to collect her scattered innards. Well-wishers came from all the neighbouring villages, al-Mantar, al-Harash, al-Qita, al-Matukh and Sufuh al-Rih. Everyone knew Salman al-Khattar, the 'chauffeur', the noblest, handsomest, best-respected driver in the mountains. They could spot that Land Rover of his from a mile away. It was an ambulance for the sick and a coach for brides and grooms, it transported the isolated, and sheltered the aimless and those between paths. Salman was an adventurer: he had a legend and a woman waiting in every hamlet, and in every town some pals to play cards with or to smoke hash, which grew in abundance in the volcanic soil until the Revolutionary Government got involved. They uprooted everything and planted wheat instead. Salman still knew how to get his hands on 'God's high' though, which was what they called a joint.

The men got drunk. They danced the Dabke and emptied whole clips into the air. Endless bursts from automatic rifles, 75mm and Baker and Makarov pistols peppering the sky. In a country that'd been defeated before the war had even begun, their repressed, unavenged manhood was on display for history's sake; they still had their self-respect, you know, even after the Six Day 'Setback' in this village, which had absolved a young woman's beastly slaughter. After the pseudo-gun salute, the feast began.

Five separate fights were stamped out, and they would've ruined the party had it not been for Umm Salman, her relatives' steel nerves and her advance planning. She'd taken eleven young men aside and gave them each five lire to stay sober – no drink, no hash – for the whole party. She gave them strict instructions, which can be easily summarised: If anyone makes trouble, throw them the hell out – but don't make a scene. If necessary, take them into the barn where we feed the cattle, tie them up and let them sleep it off.

The party went off without a hitch, and the marriage too, was consummated without complication. A white banner, dappled with nine drops of blood, flapped in the breeze, announcing a deflowering that had been some time coming. The final harvest produced eleven drunk and stoned, who were locked up in Fadila al-Khattar's hay store. They were set free the next morning.

Farida's family missed the party. Not a single relative turned up, even though the al-Khattars had sent an invitation. To tell the truth, there wasn't anyone in al-Manabi to send: her father had been killed in a fight with a Bedouin, her mother had married an emigrant and moved to Brazil, and her uncle, in whose house she'd been brought up, harboured all sorts of resentment as her father had left him with debts, which he was still paying off. As far as he was concerned, the girl's mother was a whore who'd slept with every man in the mountains until she finally got a blind man to marry her and left the country.

Farida had returned the favour, though, repaying the family all she'd cost them in an instant. She'd given them back everything they'd lost with a noble gesture that they just didn't understand at the time. She'd been raised in that house but they'd always treated her like a servant. After the disaster of their loss to Salman, her uncle Muaz and his relatives were ready to forget all about those three nights and they hoped desperately that the Land Rover driver would keep all that had happened a secret. They didn't come to the party. Rather they disappeared from her life altogether.

On the second night of the wedding, she swam in a magical halo. Her eyes rang with mystery, passion and an intoxicating coquetry. Salman had been good to her. He let her taste the body's splendours slowly at first, counting on many repeats. He let it happen gently and only after he'd first celebrated with her, lavished her with gifts and irresistible affection.

Sarmada was overwhelmed by the al-Khattar family's generous hospitality and decided to pay it back the next night. Families of well-wishers came from all the neighbouring villages and they

contributed to an astounding feast studded with huge trays of croquettes and supple sheep's heads. Ghee flowed without end and
magazine after magazine of bullets flashed in the sky. As the party
raged, a 1947 SIG pistol was loaded and fired into the air, but then
it suddenly jammed in the hands of one of the guests, a member of
the al-Qazzaz family. The young men of Sarmada sniggered at the
pistol no one had ever heard of and at the stranger-guest whose
embarrassment was more than he could bear. His manhood was
on the line! He couldn't manage to fix the jam that had stalled the
final bullet, and rather than take care of it later, he started trying
to yank the bullet out of the blasted chamber frantically – with
the barrel pointed at the crowd. Fadila had the presence of mind
to walk up and point the barrel toward the ground, but before she
could reach it, the bullet shot out, straight through her right hand,
whizzing over the head of one of the children who was busy collecting empty cartridges, singeing Umm Numan's headscarf and
Buthayna the groom's sister's shawl, and ending up in Salman al-
Khattar's chest; he'd only just returned to his seat beside the bride
after leading a whirlwind round of happy Dabke dancing. He died
on the spot.

The boisterous wedding party turned into a blood-soaked
funeral, and Farida had to live with the mark of ill omen from
that day forth. The great dread that would envelop Sarmada in the
coming days had begun.

❧

The villagers took turns inviting me over; each had something to
add and something to cover up. Some of the local dignitaries were
getting on in years and I seemed to make them feel young again. I
listened closely and put the story together the way the village told
it to me. It beggared belief: Farida's death hadn't actually buried
Sarmada's secrets, on the contrary, everybody wanted to come
clean all of a sudden. For the first time ever, I'd come upon a story

that everybody agreed on. Let me paint the picture for you now. I promise not to butt in.

I turned on my mobile and found a text from work and another from a friend of mine in Damascus who said he'd been expecting me for several days now. There was a message from Azza Tawfiq, too. She teased me affectionately and said she'd been dreaming about Sarmada every night since we'd met. She was dying to come see the place for herself she said and she begged me to hurry up as her curiosity was killing her. I replied, telling her that my own curiosity was about to cost me my job and that Hela Mansour was still in Sarmada's heart, still alive in shattered memories. I turned off the phone as I walked up to Raifeh's house. A few old women who claimed they'd been friends with Hela and Farida had got together there and they took it in turns to tell me the story of the mythical torment that plagued the village in the days following the wedding.

After the forty days of mourning were up, Farida found she didn't have a lot of options: she could either stay in Sarmada and face her fate or she could go back to nowhere. The al-Khattar family just watched her spitefully, and as their feelings of hurt and loss grew, she began to hear muttered suggestions that she ought to leave and return to her own family. Shaykh Farouq came to see her and asked her gruffly about her 'plans', but the message was clear. She wasn't welcome in that house any longer and it was time to get going.

The following morning, she began to pack up her things. She was getting ready to leave Sarmada, but she didn't know where for; she just knew she had to get out of that awful place. And then something happened to put her departure on hold. The cemetery opened its devilish maw and began receiving corpses. At Salman's funeral, the throng, who were pushing and shoving in their agitation, caused the coffin to teeter twice on the pallbearers' shoulders. Some of the women screamed wildly and burst into tears at the ill omen. 'Steady the coffin! Steady the coffin!'

When they brought the coffin out of the women's majlis, they danced the groom's dance as he was carried on their shoulders and the mourners all threw handfuls of rice and rose-petals into the air. They suddenly broke out in wedding songs and well-wishes and forgot all about his death, cheering him on like a groom come to fetch his bride. Sarmada and half the mountain bewailed the groom who hadn't got to enjoy his wedding day. In the days that followed, the al-Khattar family was visited by the worst spate of bad luck imaginable; it was as if some blind power had descended on Sarmada and transformed the quiet village into a senseless nightmare. The family had no end of disasters. A week after the forty-day period of mourning was over, they received news that Salman's younger brother, Saji, had been shot by a gang trying to rob his shop in Caracas. Once again, the suffering home seemed enshrouded in grief, and only a few days later, Umm Salman al-Khattar's half-sister, Samiha, was caught by a flaring bread oven fire that charred her face and left her with third-degree burns all over her body. They all hoped that she'd just die as it would've been more merciful than the excruciating pain she had to endure.

Death stalked the house and wove its sticky web about the unhappy family. In a moment, it could strike or just skirt past. At another, its sickle would randomly cut down young men in the prime of their lives, just because they were connected to the family in some way. Slowly but surely, death bolstered its presence, and even began to round up those who'd taken the al-Khattar's side and paid them a visit. As one group of mourners was leaving the house, a tornado blew in from the north, scattering plastic bags and dust, obscuring sight and knocking down Abu Muhammad Qasim's barn. The tornado then lifted a zinc panel off the roof of the village patrol and sliced Samih al-Ali's neck with it. The offering of condolences became a funeral in its own right. Salih Korkmaz, Khazim Wahhab, Murad Qamar al-Din and Radwan Massa were all killed in horrific accidents after going to the doomed al-Khattars to pay their respects. Suspicions were also

raised about Juwayda al-Jarazi: she choked to death on her own
tongue not long after she'd sent some food over to the al-Khattar house to help feed their condoling guests; and so she too was
added to the list of fatalities.

෴

'You centipede! You scorpion! You crow! You owl!' Umm Salman
and her daughter Buthayna hurled all those slurs at Farida along
with many more, exhausting every entry in the dictionary of ill
omens. The friends who'd come to commiserate all agreed, though
there were fewer of them now. Faced with the tyrannical force
of death, assigning blame allowed people to confront its caprice.
A simple – or simplified – cause helped them accept the greater
wisdom that cut lives short and how strange its choices seemed.
Eventually, Umm Salman ran out of tears: she'd cried so much and
for so long without any interruption. As her tears dried up, her
breasts began to swell with every new calamity until she needed
two men to help her carry them when she went to the toilet. They
grew so large she couldn't get through the door anymore and
Saeed the blacksmith brought her a wheelbarrow to help her move
around. The various remedies that the herbalists prescribed failed
to halt their inexplicable growth and the village's resident nurse,
whom everyone called Doctor Salem regardless, told them to take
her to the hospital in Damascus. It was a condition that neither
modern nor ancient medicine had ever encountered before.

Raifeh told me that she'd felt the breasts with her own two
hands. They were filled with liquid, she said. The milk sloshing
around inside sounded like a waterwheel. Poor Umm Salman was
consumed with the hardships the Lord had sent to test her and she
stubbornly refused to go to any hospital and let some stranger put
his hands on her body, not even if her breasts got as big as hot-air
balloons!

'It's a punishment for something she did in a past life that she must have been pretty damned proud of.' That was how Shaykh Farouq began and then he asked the other shaykhs to pray for Umm Salman al-Khattar and to ask God to release her from the bonds of her affliction. They recited passages from the Holy Epistles of Wisdom; the shaykh had chosen 'Crushing the Heretic' and 'Bearing the Truth' and they read them with profound humility and chanted. Late Thursday night, two of the shaykhs brought her a bowl of water, over which they'd read the necessary prayers and asked Umm Salman to reaffirm her faith. She repeated the Covenant of the Faithful over and over and declared her submission to her destiny as a woman of pure Druze blood, no matter what shape it took.

As she drifted off, somewhere between being asleep and awake, five horsemen appeared before her eyes. They were each a different colour, lined up before a gate and shielding her from fate's whims. She had a sudden epiphany: these were the five cosmic principles who'd taken human form and established the Druze doctrine. They represented Reason, Soul, Utterance, Precedent and Consequent. According to Druze teachings, they would appear from behind a great wall on the Day of Resurrection and free the earth from the False Messiah and bring all humankind to Egypt to be judged. Then she watched as they galloped toward the distant horizon and faded away. But her anguish returned the next morning, sharper than ever and culminated in a ceaseless, tearless scream.

As Death came and went, along with a steady stream of tears and prayers from the church and the majlis, Farida could only hide in silence from the dry-eyed crying and a painful grief that wouldn't let up. She had a vision in her sleep, or she dreamt something that startled her awake in the morning. She went into the bathroom and saw the late Salman's razor lying in front of the mirror. She took it and steeled her nerves. She entered Umm Salman's bedroom and walked straight up to those barrel-sized breasts. She undid the woman's nightgown as Umm Salman merely watched with reddened eyes and a knotted tongue, imploring the crazy bitch to get the hell away. She summoned all her strength and lashed out at Farida: 'Get away from me! Leave me alone!' She began to shout: 'Where the hell is everybody?'

Farida glared at her and held the blade up against her throat. 'Shut up. Not another word … I'm warning you.'

Umm Salman was paralysed with fright as she watched Farida take a nipple in her hands and make two perpendicular cuts with the razor like a plus sign. Poor swollen-breasted Umm Salman started to scream as if she were possessed, but Farida's cruel hands paid her no attention. She waited and when nothing came out, she bent down and began to suck on the nipple as hard as she could. She could taste the milky grief as it spurted into her mouth and on her face. The peculiar sweetness gave her a shiver. Then she did the same thing to the other breast.

She left Umm Salman whimpering, her grief flowing out in the milk and ran to get as many containers from the kitchen as she could. She collected twenty bottles and half a bucket's worth of the blue-tinged liquid over the next two hours. By midday, the people of Sarmada – Druze, Christian and Muslim – had all gathered to see the miracle. The massive swelling had come down and her breasts were back to normal; by sunset, Umm Salman was on her feet to greet the guests who'd come to congratulate her on beating the curse. Everyone had been affected by the mysterious burden that had struck Umm Salman and her family. It had taken her sister, her only two sons, cousins and a whole host of guests; it paralysed two of the neighbours, gouged out the eye of another, and caused no end of trouble for the people of Sarmada who were too afraid to speak out in the midst of invisible, unpredictable Death. But now, it seemed, the curse had begun to lift. The villagers greeted the next morning with the knowledge that better days – happier, less painful days – were in store for them. They'd waited the whole night for any sign of continued foreboding from out of the rocky wasteland and the surrounding wilderness, but nothing came – nothing but a resounding silence with occasional cricket-chirps. The jackals that had hounded Sarmada with portents of impending evil throughout had fallen silent at last.

The neighbours didn't have to stuff their ears with tree sap and cotton wool when they went to bed to block out the mixed cacophony of Umm Salman's wailing and the menacing jackal howls. Umm Salman hugged Farida tightly the next morning. 'God bless you, my daughter. How can I ever repay you?'

'For what, mother?' Farida asked, all the love in the world radiating from her face. 'I don't want anything except to see you well,' she said, and then softly added: 'Just let me go live in the shed.'

'What shed are you talking about, Farida?'

'Princess' shed next door.'

'As you wish. You're family now, my daughter', she said, submitting to a gentle sob embroidered with a clear thread of salty, colourless tears.

Farida set about moving her things into the shed straightway. The shed belonged to Salman al-Khattar's family and it was really just a small barn where they kept the cattle. Its last resident had been Princess, the daring cow who met her demise at the bottom of the cliff not far from the Salt Spring. Umm Salman had given her her blessing, but Buthayna, her sister-in-law until a stray bullet killed her husband, had only curses for her. Buthayna felt she had to go see the men of the family to get them to do something about this madness. When they came to object, Umm Salman just stood her ground. 'What I do with my inheritance is my business.'

She got the village elder to come witness the sale contract; she sold the shed to Farida for one Syrian lira – that was all. Farida wandered around her new home, carefully checking it out: there were two rooms under a mud ceiling propped up by seven beams stolen off the Hejaz railway line. The roof was made out of sugar cane stalks and planks of wood resting on stone arches and the walls desperately needed to be white-washed again. There was a place to store straw out the front and enough room for a veranda or a sizable garden. She rolled up her sleeves and started cleaning the place up tirelessly. Only a few weeks later, the rank old barn surged with life and, for some reason, many of the neighbours had lent a hand; the place was as good as new. Once it was fit to live in, Farida went to thank Umm Salman for her generosity.

'You've got to take all of my dear departed son's furniture. It's yours by rights.'

'God bless you', Farida said, kissing her mother-in-law's brow and hands. Now she had a home.

Umm Salman turned and went into her room, where the walls were covered with the pictures of the dead and there was one of Shaykh Jalil standing in front of five horses, each a different colour. She remained there for many years, cut off from society, free to worship God and mourn her departed children and relations, until she became divorced from reality and moved into a permanent limbo that she only ever left once: on her way to the Khashkhasha cemetery in a solemn funeral procession.

Farida followed her visions and vague intuition. She wanted to be independent but also to belong, and it seemed she'd finally got what she'd wanted. She took the bottles she'd filled with grief-milk pouring out of Umm Salman's breasts and found a place for them in the shed. She wrapped them in hessian and buried them among the damp and brittle straw husks. She realised it was best to keep them out of the sun and reasonably cool. She turned half of the milk into cheese, which she soaked in brine, and the other half she distilled as you would wine. She used the skills she'd learnt distilling grapes in her village of al-Manabi and patiently performed what time had shown was best: to keep it in a cool, dark place until she could figure out what the essence of the substance was: blessing or curse?

She took a bottle of the grief-milk and examined it. She carefully took off the lid and sniffed: it was pungent and perfumed. Her skin broke out in gooseflesh and the very roots of her hair trembled. A vague fear filled her and she nearly thought about throwing the whole lot away, but then she decided she'd give it time.

As she walked back to the storeroom, her foot slipped and the bottle fell. The white, blue-tinged milk spilled all over the ground. She picked up the scattered shards of glass with the ill omen of the spilled milk renting her heart. The liquid flowed down into the middle of the garden. She hosed the area down, prayed for protection against the Devil, and engrossed herself once more in planting pots of basil, oleander and damask rose.

On the spring morning of 9 March 1969, you could say that she nearly fainted when she saw that the plants that had soaked up the spilt milk were green, unlike any she'd seen before. Their wafting scent was like a longing mingled with delicate pity and as the fruit, bud and flower-laden branches swung in the spring breeze, Farida was bewitched by the soft, whispering rustle they made; it was like the song of wailing mourners. It stirred hearts and rescued the names of deceased and absent friends as the unique and unfamiliar perfume filled the air.

Farida shook her head from left to right, trying to clear out the mysterious images that had populated her morning and invoked the name of God. Then she listened once more, though now she heard nothing but a whirring whisper. 'You're losing it, Farida', she muttered to herself. She waved to her neighbour: 'Good morning, Abu Khalid!' It was none other than Salama.

'It certainly is a good morning', he replied, adding 'Praise the Lord who made you, you vision', under his breath.

She went on with her work, spurred by the puzzle of the plants and the rustling of desire for something unknown, whose mysterious pigments had begun to tint her whole existence. She built a low, stone wall around the garden and planted cypress trees and cactuses along the perimeter. Out of that square plot, she'd created an arousing oasis of shrubs, trellises and flower beds filled with basil, oleander, jasmine and damask rose. She tended the morning glory and storksbills that climbed the walls until the garden became a dark grove perfectly suited to her own shrouded isolation.

Nine months after moving into the shed, she decided she finally had to do something about the endless stream of suitors, courters and give-it-a-triers. She needed to find a suitable husband who'd protect her from the vulnerability of solitude and agree to marry her without any fuss or big celebration. One day, Aboud al-Dari, or Aboud Scatterbrains – as the people of Sarmada affectionately called him – came to propose. Farida's only condition was that she could stay at the shed and that he would have to come and live with her. They read from the Quran to make the engagement official; the wedding would take place in a month's time.

Once the well-wishers had all left, Aboud just sat there, his round, wheat-brown face etched with bashfulness. He had big eyes which gave off an innocence and benevolence that didn't quite fit his giant's figure. His bulky fingers were scarred and bruised from his daily battle with bricks: he was the most talented builder in the village and for miles around. He'd turned down the chance to go abroad, not swayed by the invitation to join his two brothers in Venezuela. He'd built his own house, stone by stone out of the ruins of a Roman temple. He'd saved the best rocks for the walls, cutting and shaping them with his uncommon skill.

Aboud Scatterbrains told Farida how he felt in two sentences: 'The day I saw you step out of Salman's Land Rover – God rest his soul – I couldn't sleep all night. My life didn't begin until the day you agreed to marry me and the shaykhs read the Quran for us.' Farida smiled but said nothing. Aboud wished her a nice evening and left the discomfiting silence for home.

He didn't come the next morning to take her shopping for the things they needed, as he'd promised. Instead she heard news of him: He's dead. It was heart failure, most likely.

'Hold on. Hold it right there – Let's stop for a second,' I interrupted the man telling the story. 'Hold on, there's no need to embellish here. Did you just make that up? You can't be serious.'

The man looked at me, leaving aside for a moment the important task of choosing the precise words. 'Why's it so hard to believe that Aboud Scatterbrains went to bed and never woke up? He asphyxiated. He up and had a heart attack in the prime of life. You know, a little emotion can melt away cold reason. If you just listen and pay attention, you'll discover how ridiculous death is, how cheap. Why would I lie? I'm supposed to be telling you the facts, not trying to win your approval at the expense of an undeniable reality that doesn't hurt anybody. I've got everything I need to change the story as I wish – to add or omit, create or destroy. What can you possibly have against an honest and serene death in the night?

'Would it have been better if a rabid dog had run up and bit Aboud on the leg? Would that seem more plausible to you? Who cares if he died? Or went abroad? Or committed suicide after Farida spurned him? Or maybe he got killed while hunting or drowned while swimming down at the pond? Or what if he'd married Farida and lived happily ever after? Anything's possible, anything could have easily happened. But it didn't. And you know why? Because Aboud went to bed that night and never woke up. He developed a clot and his heart stopped.'

Memories were awoken again a year after the wedding. Farida became the black widow once more, an ill-omened murderess, because Sarmada had an imagination, after all, just like any other village in the world. You were always bumping up against mysteries and miracles and genies and secret powers. It didn't take much to build the foundation for the meaninglessness of life out of the dry dust of legends.

The man telling the story asked me to be quiet and he uprooted anything in my mind that might have kept the truth out, anything that might have kept the truth of what had happened, and what was yet to happen, from getting in. He dropped me back into the world of Sarmada where events take place according to its mood, paying no attention to the rules of novels.

Farida met the outcry surrounding Aboud Scatterbrains' death with silence. She shut her windows and withdrew, surrendering herself to insuperable waves of sadness and deep feelings of disgrace and solitude. She was cursed, she felt, and there was no one there to cushion her fall, no one to lean on. She didn't attend the funeral, which was the source of much village anxiety, lest it mark the beginning of another spate of fatalities. Everyone thought it best to bury the deceased quickly and to return straight home to await the jackals' howling in the distant rocky wasteland.

Yet Buthayna, her former husband's sister, couldn't stand it any longer and she flew into a rage. She grabbed a can of petrol and attacked Farida's shed. She soaked the door and courtyard and then set it alight, shrieking curses on the wicked, evil witch inside. She kept shouting, 'Get out of here! Leave us alone! Leave us alone, you crow!' until her cousins came and dragged her back to the house. Farida, trapped inside the house, crouched in a corner, wrapped herself in a thick woollen blanket, and sobbed without end. She woke with a start after a sudden blackout and ran to the kitchen. She grabbed a knife and made a deep gash across her forearm; blood came gushing out.

'Forgive me, Lord! Forgive me though I don't know what I've done to deserve your wrath!' She wailed as she fell to the ground.

Salama saved her. He'd come over to pay his respects and cheer her up. He, for one, didn't like the idea of her bearing the blame for something that obviously wasn't her fault. And if she truly was cursed and prey to fate, well then that wasn't her fault either. It plagued him that she had no support, no family, nobody. He was distraught, but his wife, Umm Khalid, just kept repeating the same old curses, the same old poison against that 'unholy chameleon!'

He arrived at Farida's place and knocked. He waited. 'Farida?' he called. 'Open up.' No answer. He thought about going back home, but then he saw a thin stream of blood trickle out from under the gate. He knocked down the gate and found her, nearly dead.

She finally woke up, and with a little tender care from Salama and his newly compassionate wife, she recovered quickly. Her health improved, but she lost that arresting smile and she moved more ploddingly now. Her spirit sank deeper into the abyss of a grief that couldn't be remedied. She had to find a way to protect herself from want, and from the twisting corridors of emptiness and suffering. Nothing was better for it than tending her plants and her stash of grief-milk, extracting essential oils from flower petals and sesame seeds, making her own dusky-tasting wine and discovering plant secrets. She took some bottles of the blue-grey grief milk she'd stored and began to run some experiments, many of which she'd learnt as a child; she was the daughter of a herbalist who'd been fascinated by plants and their power to heal the sick.

She sniffed the grief-milk and found it smelt ever so faintly rancid with an underlying sweetness. She poured some into a copper saucepan and brought it to a boil, stirring in a handful of nigella seeds and some honey from the mountains. As soon as it started boiling, she sprinkled in a roux of flour and ghee. She rolled the resulting mixture into small knuckle-sized balls and wrapped them in cellophane like bonbons. She poured herself half a glass of homemade buttermilk and drank it down with one of her little bonbons. She licked up the clotted trail at the side of her mouth and instantly her stomach began to cramp. Her body went into spasms, she clenched her teeth, poured with sweat, and dissolved into a fit of violent sobbing unlike any she'd ever known. She wanted to call out for help, but no sound came. She curled up on the floor, writhing and twitching, until she finally lost consciousness.

She came to that evening. She hurried over to the mirror and saw that her face was uncommonly white, smooth and refreshed. Stranger still, her spirits soared and her heart seemed full of laughter; she felt wonderfully happy. She realised at that moment that it was her duty to reawaken joy in the village, which was surrounded by sorrow, stones and dark blue basalt.

To double check the substance's extraordinary effects, she decided to test it again on a woman from the al-Hamid family. The woman was suffering from the pain of a crushing loss. All her dreams had become recurring nightmares since her husband and son had heartlessly immigrated to some country in Latin America whose name she could never quite remember. She'd heard nothing from them ever since Saji had been killed in Caracas. Farida sat down beside the woman, Khoza al-Hamid, who'd started working as a hired mourner at funerals to heat the frigid ones up a little. Her heart-breaking ballads caused previously held-back tears to pour out and made the families feel like they'd given their loved one a fitting send-off. And she got some money for her trouble. Farida gave her one of the bonbons she'd made and told her to chew it. Farida's heart began to throb as she watched the woman's face contort in pain and go dark red. She was sweating and gasping for breath. The woman's daughter came in and screamed: 'What have you done to my mother, goddamn you?!' Farida would have wavered had she not felt that what was needed now was a little patience.

With feigned composure, she gestured to the girl to quiet down, and when calm gestures failed, she shouted back, 'Be quiet!'

After a helpless hour, the red mask cleared and the woman began to sob uncontrollably. She was crying for every year of her life, for all that she'd longed for and all that she'd lost. For two straight hours, she writhed and groaned and screamed and pleaded as all the toxins of her heart were gathered up and expelled through her eyes. Her body now only gently rose and fell. She was refreshed little by little and her breathing became more regular. Her face glowed tranquilly. Her voice was lilting, and though it was still drenched in grief, it had an arresting grace.

'What did you give me, Farida?' the woman asked innocently.

'Medicine, dear,' replied Farida, confident and soothing. 'You ought to be able to rest easy now.'

'It's like a weight's been lifted off my chest,' the woman said.

Farida put the bedcovers over her and kissed her brow. 'Go to sleep now. I'll come check on you tomorrow.'

'God bless you. Thank you for everything.'

'Don't mention it.' Before she left, Farida turned to the woman's daughter and said, 'Send for me if anything happens.' Though she had no clue what, if anything, she could do if something actually were to happen. She said it only to inspire the still-suspicious daughter's confidence, and to remind herself that she was now sworn to a greater duty, which she couldn't ignore.

ॐ

Now that she'd managed, with her happy heart and winning smile, to regain nearly everyone's trust and made them forget all about that 'cursed woman' talk, Farida started making preparations for a rice pudding party. She'd become famous throughout Sarmada and the surrounding area as a talented herbalist, though she'd still failed to win over Buthayna, her slain husband's sister. While Farida was making preparations for her feast, Buthayna was still consumed by her hatred and envy of this satanic outsider. After more than a few days' hesitation, she paid a secret visit to the famous soothsayer of Kanakir. 'I want Farida's heart to burn', she said, 'like mine did when my brother died. I want her to suffer. I want her to get a taste of what she's put us through.'

'Are you absolutely certain she's the cause of all the suffering in the village?' the soothsayer asked.

'She's the cause for all that and more. I'm a million per cent certain. Ever since she came to Sarmada we've had nothing but death and bad luck.'

The soothsayer warned her that the spell wouldn't work if Farida was innocent.

'At least I'd know then that she was,' Buthayna quipped.

'Okay, as you wish.' The soothsayer consented indifferently. She agreed to prepare the amulets for driving out evil in exchange for a

21-karat gold ring, a ram with a broken horn, and an eighth-kilo of the choicest raisins. Buthayna handed over the ring and the raisins and promised to bring the ram after the job was done. The sooth-sayer told her she also needed one of Farida's nightgowns, which Buthayna had no trouble getting among the things Farida had left at their house, and she also got her mother's name and her date of birth from the marriage certificate for the soothsayer, along with several other silly things she asked for. Buthayna, though, took the soothsayer's instructions very carefully: she brought everything the soothsayer had requested. The soothsayer then set about cre-ating the most powerful spell she could, with help from the secrets contained in the pages of Abdullah al-Hazred's *al-Azif*.

As the full September moon shone in the sky above, the sooth-sayer withdrew to her private chamber and unlocked the ancient chest. She carefully removed and unwrapped the book of death's secrets, known as *al-Azif*. She admired the binding made from the tanned flesh of people who'd died in horrific accidents and illustrations made with needles. She remembered the advice her father repeated every time he read a chapter from the book to her, revealing the secrets of death: 'Never use this book unless it's abso-lutely necessary.'

She analysed Farida's name with geomancy and discovered that she was, in fact, a descendant of one of the twenty lost angels, who were sent to Earth when it was created to help organise the environment and to help humans arrange their work so that they would have a specific mission in life. Twenty of these angels forgot their original allegiance and refused to return to Heaven when called by God. The Earth had seduced them and in its deficiency they'd discovered that eternity is frightening and painful. So they disobeyed the divine warning and married members of this mis-guided, inconsequential mortal species. Their descendants were a plague upon the earth for they had inherited a corrupted, ran-corous, jealous nature. And when their waywardness reached the point of no return, God twice ordered that they be destroyed: once when he wiped out Iram of the Pillars and once with Noah's flood. Now it was true that the descendants of the Twenty had lost much of their powers, but they continued to transmigrate and become reborn, and they carried on from one generation to the next, infiltrating human society, undetected by all but those who possessed the knowledge of The Names of the Dead, which the author called *al-Azif*.

The soothsayer searched for the right spell, invoking the help of a giant demon-servant, a direct descendant of the genie who'd gobbled up the author of the book in a Damascus alley some 1,300 years before. She took the book in her trembling grasp, unaware that it was the last existing Arabic copy of one of the most controversial texts in history. *Al-Azif*, or the *Necronomicon*, is over 900 pages long and divided into seven chapters. It was written by a Yemeni poet called Abdullah al-Hazred – which, perhaps, is a corruption of Hadramaut – who wrote it after many years of solitude spent in the desert hunting the few powerful, if ostracised, genies and demons left on earth. They, the genies and demons, had been around a long time back before God decided to cast them out and replace them with humankind, for whom he had a special affection. Al-Hazred, also known as the Mad Poet, had written a history of the deep past, filled with rich details, which hardly troubled rational thinkers and those who judged their own five senses to be sufficient. He dedicated his peculiar life to searching for the legendary ruins of Iram and symbols of antediluvian worlds hidden here on Earth. He named his book *al-Azif*, after the noises insects make in the night: the voices of genies and demons.

Abdullah al-Hazred's tragic demise put an end to his search for the descendants of the Twenty before he could complete it. In a Damascus market, a giant genie suddenly appeared right in front of him and bit off his head. The people in the market just watched in horror as the genie devoured his body piece by piece and from that day on, they couldn't stop trembling; they called this new illness epilepsy or 'the point of seizure'. And it was at this 'point', that the veil obscuring human vision was finally pulled away, or rather that the formerly invisible expanses of the mind were revealed, and the victims saw that the void is actually filled with the dead and the mutilated, with genies, demons and other creatures, and that the mind would never be the same.

The book was full of supernatural wisdom that contained the key to life and the meaning of death. Incredible truths, such as that although the Earth actually rotates clockwise, some obstacle in our minds makes us think that time progresses from east to west. No amount of explaining or pleading can change the minds of the hoi polloi. *Al-Azif* explains that we are actually looking toward the past and not the future. The so-called future has happened already and it's the past that is yet to come. This is where religions get their dogged assurance about what is to come and it is the root of a great error because the future has already happened and we are retrogressing in time. Only a few people have discovered this fact, but they don't share the great secret because the average person wouldn't be able to bear the shocking truth.

To the rational observer, the secrets of the book seem like no more than mere legends and tricks based on fundamental misunderstandings of the nature of time, but to anyone who possesses the gift of the sixth sense, and whose brain cells are not so easily duped by the other senses, the book is all truth. It is the knowledge, similar to the cosmic unity, about all that has taken place, or to put it more accurately, all that has yet to take place. Whoever possessed it, possessed the key to understanding all supernatural occurrences, prophecies and events throughout history. Yet those who owned incomplete or faulty copies were certain to suffer the most excruciating deaths imaginable. There was one copy in the Vatican, but it was incomplete and the priests were forbidden from reading it anyway. The original Arabic copy had been lost for centuries. It had once belonged to a Jewish family in Damascus, but they had it translated into Hebrew, and when they left for Palestine, they left the Arabic original with a silversmith called George Sahtout.

George Sahtout, the silversmith, had a clandestine affair with a Christian woman from the Hauran region for a long time and in 1954, after his wife died – from choking on an oversized piece of quince – they got married. Before he died, he gave his daughter a chest, which contained countless antique bracelets and a necklace of emeralds and other precious gems, which were said to have once belonged to Bilqis, the famed Queen of Sheba. The chest also contained a mysterious book, filled with symbols for deciphering the secrets of the dead and bringing them back to life, and ways of commanding occult forces and invisible creatures to do one's bidding. The silversmith had taught his daughter, Sara, who later became known as the soothsayer of Kanakir, the secrets of the symbols and he left her the book so that she could study it closely over the years to come.

Relying on all her training, the soothsayer wrote out a revenge-curse on talismans with soot she made from the following ingredients: she burnt a piece of lizard tail, which carried on twitching for hours, and when it finally fell still, she added some black pepper and a hyena's molar and ground it all up into a powder with some murderous ink she'd made from the skull of a stranger who'd burned to death – she'd dug up his grave and used his bones to make ashes that incited the dead's contempt for the living. With this soot, she traced symbols and letters and conjured up strange names and illnesses to torment Farida so that she'd leave Sarmada and never come back.

She slipped the amulets into Buthayna's trembling hand and also gave her back the ring and the ram. 'Kill the ram', the soothsayer said, 'but don't let any humans eat the meat. Give it to the wild animals who live in the wasteland. All I want is for that she-devil to leave the village.' She gave the girl a phial of arsenic tincture and told Buthayna to wait for a week and that if the spell didn't work, to pour a few drops of the liquid onto Farida's food. Once it reached her stomach, she would lose all her evil powers.

Buthayna took the amulets and the phial, unaware that she was actually carrying a deadly poison, enough to kill a large camel.

Farida wanted to convince the Mansour brothers to come to her party, so she decided she'd just go over there and invite them herself. She put on a lovely, embroidered dress that showed off her lightly bouncing cleavage, and even a little lipstick. She covered her hair with a gauzy scarf and brushed her long locks down across her shoulders. She made up a platter of croquettes and a pot of bulgar boiled with chunks of meat, and set off toward the old mill.

They were surprised to see her, to put it lightly. All five brothers were out in the field beside the house, hoeing the soil, so she set the things she'd brought down on the stone window sill and called to them. They stopped their work and eyed the strange woman curiously. Shafee, the youngest brother who was all of eighteen, had a twinkle in his eye as he walked toward her and smiled.

'Where do you think you're going?' His eldest brother Nawwaf called after him gruffly.

'To see who she is, and what she wants,' he answered and carried on in her direction. He greeted her and had the feeling that he was seeing a creature from another planet. Something flew up out of the cage of his soul, which burst open and seemed as if it would never be closed again. The bitter veil that had covered his almond, endlessly questioning eyes disintegrated.

'What's your name?' she asked, velvet-voiced.

'Shafee. Shafee Mansour.'

'Wonderful. I actually came over to introduce myself and to invite you all to come for rice pudding at my place. You and your brothers, the night after tomorrow, on the Feast of the Cross.'

'Oh, but we can't!' said Shafee. She stared into his eyes. He felt that some strange bliss was sliding along that gaze and down into his soul, shaking him to the core. He didn't want it to end, but it did:

'No, but you can come', she said.

'I'd love to. I'll try.'

'Shafeeeeee!' Nawwaf's hoarse, angry voice brought him back to his senses, and back out to stone-hoeing in the fields.

'I'll be waiting for you', said Farida seductively, and then she turned and walked away.

Naturally, there wasn't a force in the world – not Nawwaf, or Nayef, or Talal, or Shahir, or all four brothers shouting at once – who could unglue Shafee's eyes from her bottom as he watched it dance beneath her floral dress.

৯৯

She needed help from the neighbours if she was going to pull off a real feast of rice pudding, grape molasses sweets and pancakes dipped in the blue-tinged grief-milk, which would feed all of Sarmada and advertise her skills as an expert herbalist. She bought three sacks of rice and borrowed ten cans of milk, and then made the crumbly cakes out of grape molasses, ghee and flour. Some of the women took it upon themselves to tidy up the garden. Farida had borrowed chairs from the primary school so that the party could be extended out into the clearing in front of her house. It took the women two whole days to prepare for the party, during which time Buthayna came over, accompanied by Umm Khalid, to make up with Farida – sinisterly masking her true intentions. Farida could hardly believe it and she welcomed Buthayna like a sister. As Farida and the other women prepared for the big celebration, Buthayna monitored her anxiously. She saw her drink occasionally from a bottle of milk wrapped in hessian to keep it cool, which she'd set down next to the water butt. Buthayna made sure no one was looking and then she poured a few drops of the soothsayer's tincture into the bottle. She made an excuse about having something urgent to take care of, and off she went.

As the rice boiled away in several large cauldrons, Farida took the hessian-wrapped bottle and poured it into the cans of milk. She stirred them up well, ever certain that the substance she'd drawn from Umm Salman's breasts would soon cure all of Sarmada of its pain. She poured out the whole bottle and then she boiled the milk, before adding it to the fluffy and bubbling rice. This she flavoured with orange-blossom water and spices that spurred an appetite for life as well as for food.

The evening of 27 September was a turning point in the history of Sarmada. The village desperately needed someone who could restore a little life to the sad, scared place. Even laughter had come to be seen as a sin and the villagers prayed to God to keep them safe whenever someone let a foolhardy chuckle slip. After they'd seen how death could change a happy wedding into an unstoppable wave of funerals, they began to believe that they simply hadn't been made to enjoy life, or even to live it. There was evil behind anything that made you smile, so they decided that they preferred the stoic face of safety to the laughter of punishing disaster.

Farida, though, buzzed with joy, hurrying about as if floating on a smiling cloud. She gathered all the children around and passed out sweets and jingling coins. She took advantage of their excited anticipation for the Feast of the Cross and got them to build a big bonfire in the open space in front of her house, where she'd marked out a safe space for it, and she got them to go around to all the families who weren't coming to the party, promising them plenty more paraffin, firewood and sweets.

At noon, the children ran after Atallah, the sacristan, all the way to the door of the old church. Everyone loved the witty, rash sacristan: he couldn't go a day without losing control of his tongue and then the insults would just slide off it. His last hit had been a running joke in Sarmada for weeks. When his son Michel came down with a bad case of the measles, Atallah got very worried and swore to God that he'd sacrifice one of his cows if his son got better. Two days later, the boy was on the mend, so he ran down to the barn and found his donkey laid out, dead and rigid on the floor. 'Are you getting old, now, God?' he shouted to the sky. 'You can't tell the difference between a donkey and a cow anymore?'

The children were so impatient to receive their holiday treat that the sacristan had to open the church door for them so they could wait for Father Elias. He stuck the heavy key in the lock, but it wouldn't budge. He tried turning it again, first calmly, and then again with unmistakable annoyance. He tried turning it to the left and to the right, but the lock refused to open. He was steaming; he looked right up into the sky toward He who sits on the Heavenly Throne and said, 'So what's the point of all my praying, you son of a whore?' He kicked the door and suddenly the key turned. He looked back up at the sky with a smile. 'It's obvious there's only one way to get you to do anything.'

Father Elias arrived a few minutes later, dividing a box of peppermints among the children and recounting the story of the Feast of the Cross as he did every year. 'The Feast of the Cross is an old rite taken from the life of Saint Helena. One day, she had a vision and the Lord told her to go to Jerusalem to find the True Cross. Her son, the emperor Constantine, sent a 3,000 man attachment along with her and she passed through here, through Sarmada, on her way 1800 years ago. When she got to Jerusalem, she searched and searched for the cross until she finally found it – along with two others – buried beneath a rubbish dump!

'But she had to find out which of the three crosses was the True Cross on which Christ had been crucified, so she took the three crosses over to a funeral procession that happened to be passing by. They passed the first cross over the bier, but nothing happened, and then they passed the second cross over it, but again nothing happened. Then when they passed the third cross over the dead man, he came back to life and went on to become a caretaker at the Church of the Resurrection. Having found the True Cross, Saint Helena built a great fire there in Jerusalem on the fourteenth of September – which we call the Little Feast – to signal that her quest was complete. Everyone who could see the fire lit their own fires, in all the villages, towns and cities she'd come through on her journey. We lit a fire here in Sarmada, too, hundreds and hundreds of years ago and they saw it in Azra so they lit a fire, and on and on until the signal got all the way to Constantinople on the twenty-seventh of September and the emperor Constantine learnt that his mother had succeeded in finding the True Cross. That's the reason we celebrate every year with a big fire in honour of Saint Helena.' The children, inspired by the priest's entertaining story, took their sweets and coins and hurried off to prepare for the big celebration that evening.

Everything that happens in Sarmada is testimony to the power of forgetting: the meetings of the local branch of the Party, the educated young people from Damascus and their revolutionary zeal; every single one of them: the communists, nationalists, Nasserists and Baathists; the only idea anyone had was to take the defeat in the war and recast it as a 'setback'. Syria was swept up in a spirit inspired by Nasser's staying in power and the dream of pan-Arab unity. Peasants and the esoteric sects took advantage of the climate to break out of their former isolation and join in the calls for change, reform and revolution. Stillborn independence had given rise to decrepit leaders who transformed the Arab countries into entrenched dictatorships, which made Israel seem like an oasis of democracy in a desert of depraved barbarians and tyrants. Israel wanted nothing more than to keep these dictators around because its very existence depended on the Middle East remaining a patchwork of corrupt dictatorships and populations divided along sectarian lines.

Yet to Sarmadan passivity, politics seemed like it took place on a different planet. Local genius couldn't quite understand all the new terms or why people suddenly yearned to be free from economic feudalism and worn-out customs. Baathism had an easy time penetrating the mountains, including Sarmada, and the Syrian countryside more generally because it appealed to rural sensibilities: their hopes and concerns. But still it failed to permeate the spirit of the place, the specific social character; no ideology – not Baathism, nor anything else – could ever truly master the human character.

Farida, who alone knew how to make a wasteland bloom, how to take her green thumb and cheer a place up, borrowed some chairs and the women came to help sweep the open space in front of her house. They handed out servings of rice pudding, made with some of Umm Salman's grief-milk, which she'd also added to the dough for the pastries she'd prepared: olive and thyme, cheese and spinach, as well as a sweet variety. She even drafted in the children to take pastries around to the houses of the people who weren't attending the party. As people gathered, half-curious and half-keen, the party took on a happy mood and something like a zest for life bubbled up to the surface, albeit tentatively at first. Then Nour al-Din picked up his flute and started playing and more than thirty young men got to their feet automatically and began to dance the Dabke. When Hasoun the drummer turned up with his famous darbuka, the party was transported to a whole other level. More dancers joined the Dabke lines and everybody ate up the rice pudding and the scrumptious pastries. Sarmada celebrated warily, trying desperately to forget the nightmare of Salman's nuptials. Girls were dressed up as if they were going to a wedding and all the different local dances were performed amidst a pandemonium that spread over the entire village.

After they'd finished the tasks Farida had asked them to do, the children began going around the village, collecting cowchips, which were lumps of cow dung mixed with straw left out over the summer to dry that the villagers used to light their wood-stoves. The children's shouts could be heard throughout the village and whenever an elderly woman or a young housewife gave them several cowchips and a bottle of paraffin, they would chant:

One can, two can, can this be?
This lady here must be a queen!

But for the cheapskates who were stingy with them, they had this to say:

That's all you've got, just scraps and rags?
I'm guessing, lady, you must be a slag!

The children usually received insults against their own mothers in return, as well as several buckets of dirty water poured down from the roof.

'Holy Spawn of Satan!' shouted Shaykh Farouq when he saw the strange sweets and pastries the children had brought over and he forbade his wife and daughters from attending the 'Whore's Ball' as he liked to call it. Farida was definitely chipping away at his authority. She'd distinguished herself as a herbalist and all he had left was his special cure for the mumps: he'd scribble a few obscure phrases on swollen, lumpy faces with a ballpoint pen, recite a couple of Quranic verses, and wrap a white bandage around the patients' cartoon-like faces and tie a knot at the top of their heads. Once the patient had recovered, he'd get a chicken or some eggs for his skilful cure of the painful swelling. This had earned him the nickname 'shaykh Mumps', but the people of Sarmada never dared call him that to his face. He stormed out of his house, brandishing his cane, determined to put end to her party. When he arrived, he was appalled by the sight of the village children leaping about like monkeys, as they fed cowchips and wood into the fire. The extravagance of Sarmada's celebration absolutely shocked him. Salama had donated two sheep, which only encouraged the better-offs in the village to chip in with their own fleshy contributions, and soon the square was filled with the biggest barbecue the village had ever seen. Everyone who came brought something with them just because they wanted to contribute to the banquet and Sarmada had the time of its life. No one could have stopped the spirited exuberance that swept through the village streets. So rather than take his anger out on evil, corrupting, debauched Farida, shaykh Mumps turned around and headed back home. He sat down on the porch and called to his daughter Joumana, 'Bring me one of those pastries Farida sent over.'

'You came around just in the nick of time,' she said, handing him two pastries: one with sugar and grape molasses, the other with cheese and spinach. The shaykh took them and waved to his wife and daughters as they left for the party.

'Just don't be home late!'

A group of shaykhs came round to Shaykh Farouq's house. 'So, Shaykh … are you happy about what's going on around here?'

'Be patient, Shaykhs. The people are exhausted, let them blow off some steam.' Shaykh Farouq's large nose began to turn a pale red and his guests started devouring what pastries remained.

The party finally wound down. People were just too tired, too drunk and too danced-out and their clothes were suffused with the smoke from the big fire the children had lit; their every pore had breathed it in. The guests staggered homeward, drunk with a secret bliss. On the dusty trail leading to the graveyard, Sayil stopped and stepped off the road; he needed to relieve himself and he simply couldn't wait another moment. He listened to cicadas and crickets hissing in the night as he urinated, and with his last shakes, singeing tears began trickling out his eyes. Once he'd put himself back in order, he tried to carry on, but his eyes reddened and his tears began to stream as if he'd sniffed the most pungent onion. He couldn't explain his sudden crying fit and for some reason he didn't want it to end. He walked along the perimeter of the valley and then suddenly his stomach began to cramp and ache and his crying welled up from some unidentified pain, not because a mosquito had flown into his eye as he'd originally thought. He sat down, looking over the valley, and really began to wail.

For more than half an hour, his hot tears flowed and the sound of his blubbering reached the house nearby. Ghazi, carrying his shotgun and a lantern, walked in the direction of the sound and shouted at the weeper: 'Who's there?' Sayil couldn't stop crying and couldn't sneak off, but simply sobbed more violently than before. Ghazi shone the lantern in his face and was horrified at the sight. He dropped his pistol and set the lantern down. 'Sayil, what's wrong?' he asked, although there was no point. Sayil could only answer with more tears and louder sobbing. Ghazi grabbed him and shook him by the shoulders. He asked him again and again what was wrong – he was getting angry now – but got nothing except choked tears from the burly man wailing like a woman at the edge of the valley. Ghazi dropped his dogged interrogation and sat down beside him; he touched his eyes and felt that they, too, were wet with tears. He didn't quite know how, or why, but he began sobbing silently as well, and then sucking back the snot and moaning loudly. Ghazi's wife trembled with fear as she watched the spectres of two men in the distance, their heads between their knees, weeping, nearly howling. She couldn't decide whether to stay and comfort her horrified children or to creep cautiously down to the valley's edge and see what the hell was going on. She wiped the tears from her eyes and walked back into the house only to erupt – along with her little children – into a panic of scalding tears.

Together the two men sat there, weeping, crying as they'd never cried before. When their eyes finally dried up, Ghazi was racked with nausea and could no longer hold back the urge to bring up everything in his stomach. He vomited, followed closely by Sayil, and then together they alternated between cycles of dry sobbing and disgorging that felt it might rip their innards apart.

Behind them, there wasn't a soul in Sarmada who wasn't sobbing or throwing up; the whole village had been poisoned – though whether it was the fault of the rice pudding or the sooth-sayer's potion, no one would ever know. Young, old, those who'd attended the party, those who'd stayed at home, they all wept and vomited that night as the contagion spread from house to house. The only person who was spared both bawling and vomiting that night was Buthayna. She knew that this latest disaster was all her fault and she sat up all night in her room, listening to the weeping village. She finally nodded off at dawn and when she woke up not an hour later, she felt her eyes brimming with arrested tears, swollen, looking like pools of blood. She ran into her mother's room and found her praying, lost in the world of mourning dead, so she let her be and hurried out. The sight of the guests who'd not even made it home the night before filled her with panic as she watched them waking up, covered in vomit, laid out along the side of the road, howling in spasms. It was as if a plague had overrun the village. People were exhausted; their faces were ashen. She helped those who needed escorting home and then returned to her bedroom where she locked the door and tried, but failed, to cry until about midday when she finally fell asleep.

As Buthayna slept, mostly dreamlessly, disaster was sweeping the village. People stopped going to work they were so miserable. They sought out Shaykh Shaheen only to find him in a wretched state, squalid in his own vomit. The church door was locked and Father Elias was trying to settle his own sorrows with a mixture of herbal and camomile tea.

The village reeked. For the first time since the locals got together and built a mosque, the imam failed to perform the call to prayer because he, too, was laid low with a sour stomach and sobbing. Every time he took a sip of water, it flowed out his eyes in tears of sin. Was this heavenly rage or earthly enmity? No one really cared. All they cared about anymore was putting an end to the tears. The cramps and vomiting they'd managed to ameliorate by not eating and only drinking water and anise tea, although it instantly came back out their eyes and provoked feelings of yearning and loss that none of them had probably ever experienced. The village animals were also seized by anxiety-making premonitions like those occurring before an earthquake or natural disaster. The cows broke out of their sheds and ran off mooing wildly, followed by the village donkeys. Meowing strays broke the Sarmadans' hearts, and if they hadn't been so preoccupied with their own suffering, they'd have laughed at the dogs, who were going around as if blind-drunk and howling as if they were really their cousins, the wolves. In the rocky wasteland, a pack of hyenas linked by misfortune wrawled. Even the hens and cocks crowed at the afternoon sky and were silent at dawn. Animals foamed at the mouth and groaned, strangely, unlike anything anyone had ever heard before except out of a she-camel in heat.

Farida's prize trees and plants shared in Sarmada's vague descent into public lamentation: rose petals dissolved into drops of exquisite nectar that flowed like tears and tree-trunks burst open to ooze salty sap. Farida, who hadn't eaten any rice pudding herself, wiped at the hushed tears running down her cheeks out of guilt and horror at what was happening around her. She didn't know what to do: run away or stand her ground? She pulled herself together and tried to think of a solution. She made an herbal preparation, which helped calm her down, and began experimenting with a nettle and grief-milk infusion.

The village was wrapped in an inexhaustible gloom that bubbled up out of the heart of the earth itself – out of the soil. The mania even reached the two love-birds nesting on Farida's roof, who warbled a heart-rending song that sent anyone who heard them into a new fit of crying. Sarmada mourned. It writhed and beat its chest. The village, hollow and alone, was abandoned to its fate, left to contend with its rancour, acrimony and distress. The village was cursed but it didn't understand why. It was being punished for some mysterious crime, and there was no hope – not even the slightest shred – of being saved from its trial. The village wasn't in the least bit special; it was just an ordinary village in the east that had tried to carry on with as little change, hardship and grief as possible; without ambitions or horizons, it was content to live with as few big ideas, wants and visions as it could. They did what their intuition told them to, never getting involved in questions of fate, not once understanding why God would want to make them suffer this affliction that was more than they could bear.

On the second day of tears, groans and vomit, news of Sarmada reached the capital via three pulse traders from Deraa who'd come to buy chickpeas and lentils. They were terrified by what looked like a whole village of mourners. None of the lifeless, weeping, sighing Sarmadans would speak to them; after all, the only two people in Sarmada who could still speak were Buthayna and Farida and they were both hiding away in their bedrooms. The three traders got out of there as fast as they could and they told everyone about the unbelievable sights they'd seen. When the government heard that something serious had happened to the village, they sent forces to impose a quarantine and keep everyone out until the medical taskforce could investigate. The people of the mountains spread stories about Sarmada in fearful whispers and heaped curses on the place; they waited desperately for news.

A week later the medical taskforce arrived: an ambulance, which broke down every few miles, three doctors and a handful of nurses, who all wore gas masks, which made them look like grasshoppers or locusts and which did more to constrict their breathing than it did to protect them from the purported contamination. They entered the village anxiously and wandered around for hours, but then they quickly just wrote up their report and left. The summary of the report was no more than a couple of sentences, quoted here in full:

This is the most beautiful settlement we have ever visited in the South. The inhabitants are strikingly healthy and hale unlike any other population we have previously examined. All the rumours we received about Sarmada were total nonsense; the village *(they wouldn't even bump the village up to a 'town' in the official report)* is tranquil and safe. The residents must be some of the happiest and healthiest in the entire country. No further action required.

What had happened was that on the third day of the outbreak, Farida took drops of the antidote she'd prepared to every house in the village. All of Sarmada fell asleep at the same time and when they woke up they were cured. The plague was lifted as if it had never been, and so they rather shamefacedly set about cleaning and hosing down the absolute chaos they'd created. They were smiling again, but their faces were still a bit ashen. By the time the medical taskforce arrived, Sarmada had been up on her feet and buzzing around for days and the visitors noticed the cheerful mood of the place as they entered over Poppy Bridge. The chief physician spoke to the villagers, who denied there'd ever been a problem in the first place, and upon finding no evidence, determined there really wasn't any reason they should stay. They decided they might as well perform a routine inspection to make sure all the children in the village had been given the polio vaccine as they were already there.

Some of the villagers just couldn't keep themselves from laughing at the taskforce, who soon realised it was because of their gas masks and took them off. They went for lunch at the village elder's and they left the village touched by the serene, and ambiguous, joy of the people and by their generosity and hospitality. A few weeks later, Buthayna went back to see the soothsayer of Kanakir and she was shocked to see the woman had wasted away. The soothsayer wept constantly, collecting her glass-bead tears in several plastic bags and she threw up every single thing she ate. She flew into a hysterical panic when she saw Buthayna, but eventually calmed down long enough to explain what had happened. She gave Buthayna a chest with the seven quires of al-Hazred's book and told her to keep it in a safe place until she could find a descendant of Dahiya bint Lahiya, the Amazigh, to pass it on to – and if she couldn't find anyone, to burn the book on a Friday under a full moon. 'Watch out for that devil-spawn Farida! Look at what she's done to me. Now go, and don't ever come back.'

The soothsayer sat there waiting for her excruciating end – which came soon enough – and her village of Kanakir woke on a day in early December to find that the most talented soothsayer in all of the Hauran, had had her limbs chewed off, her eyes gouged out, her chest torn open and her heart ripped out. They burnt her house down with everything inside to try to wipe out the terror that had seized them. And the crystal tears in the plastic bags sounded as if they were screeching in horror as they exploded in the fire that consumed everything it could.

Buthayna was too young to understand; she was only twenty-one and too young to cope, but all the same she scribbled down the name of the Amazigh sorceress so she wouldn't forget it and hid the chest away in the wheat cellar without even daring to open it. She bathed herself in cold water and went into her mother's room. She threw herself on her mother's chest and pleaded for help, but her mother was in another world wandering through shadows of meaning and didn't move a muscle. She had been transported to the realm of hushed consolation with her departed loved ones where she knitted them woollen pullovers to keep them warm in the tundra of death. Buthayna wrenched the knitting from her mother's hands and pulled her arms around her, burying her head in her mother's chest. She tried to cry, but it was no use.

❧

Riyad al-Fayez found me taking photos of Farida's decaying house. He worked as a taxi driver with his brand-new 2011 Mitsubishi Lancer; his greying hair and the etched wrinkles around his eyes couldn't do anything to diminish his good-looks. 'Get in. I need to talk to you.'

I desperately wanted to make up some excuse but he opened the passenger-side door insistently. 'I want to tell you the truth about Farida.' I got in beside him. He told me about what life in Syria was like, how unbearable it'd become, and he carried on telling me about all the latest news in the world of taxi drivers until I began to regret getting into the car with him. Suddenly he pulled over to the side of the road. 'I was the first boy in Sarmada to go see Farida,' he said, and then he told me a story that confused sex with love and lies with truth. The only way I could shut him up was to turn on my mobile and go through the flood of texts I'd got. There was a text from Azza Tawfiq saying she was sorry we'd ever met and that she'd been trying to call me. I turned my mobile back off as Riyad drove and called up a bunch of his friends, telling them to come round to his house straightaway. 'You're going to get the whole story about Farida today,' he said using his cigarette to light his next one, before tossing it out the window. He sped off to introduce me to the friends he'd made as an adolescent, who were going to help me understand the strange life of that enigmatic woman.

As Farida gradually became one with her seclusion, her body grew into something between a whisper of unknown desire and the fury of dangerous cravings, which gave her cheeks a mesmerising blush. She was marked out by the secret envy of most of the other women in the village and people sensed an unusual danger coming from the green-house and its widow of misfortune. After the rice pudding party and everything else that had happened since she'd come to Sarmada, a suppressed disquiet bubbled up. People realised it was wise to keep their distance.

'*Beware the flower that buds in rubbish*', exhorted Shaykh Farouq constantly.

The men of the village openly joined in with the women's condemnation, but out of sight and in whispers, their suspicious favours continued. She was assaulted by gossiping and sharp tongues from every corner, but she simply defended her reputation with that rare smile of hers and her uncommonly sweet and inspiring demeanour.

And yet her blossoming body was of a different opinion. At night she was tormented by the feverish flames that lashed at her body, whose lifetime had been marked only by a few innocent, stolen kisses from a boy who'd rocked her fourteen-year-old world and her wedding night, during which – you might say – she'd only had the tiniest taste of the feast of the body she'd been promised and never received; her dreams of a glorious life with Salman al-Khattar had been shattered by a single stray bullet. The whole thing was like some revelation that had come to her in a strange waking-dream and completely took over her life. She didn't want to be just some hormone-soaked teenager's easy lay, but some unidentifiable impulse drove her forward toward those who still bore the last dusting of childhood, as they stood on the precipice, ready to graduate to another realm, falling into a crushing abyss of fervid desire. No one tried to understand what they were going through, they just cursed and preached.

She decided to make her body the bridge to the other side, for the crossing they were so looking forward to. She gave herself over to navigating the rugged tracks of silvery-white sexual desire, and as if by instinct, she tracked down those outcast teenagers, who'd never known a woman's body, sustained by her mysterious sweets, spiced with grief-milk now that she'd made certain that it wasn't the culprit behind the tragedy of the Feast of the Cross. She wound the first threads of her web around her first visitor, who was always passing by her shed whether or not he had a good reason. She called him over to help water the plants in her garden. She watched him: an early sprinkling of manhood above his upper lip, lust flooding his eyes every time she walked past. She gave him a sweet flavoured with mint and sesame, and thanked him breathily for his help; her gaze burning him up inside.

He never left the roof opposite her house and she expertly absorbed every sign of his agitation. She filled every one of his fifteen-year-old fantasies. Riyad al-Fayez was that first adolescent; he was her first experience through which she'd mastered everything she needed to ensure her unseen, unspoken presence – although all of Sarmada would soon come to know of it, regardless of whether she'd tried to keep it secret.

She gave him no shortage of wet dreams and he found himself masturbating whenever he had any privacy to the point that he began to look pale and drained like a skinny, big-headed sumac plant. She let him watch through the window of the shed surrounded by flowerpots and foliage as she squatted in front of the washbasin, intentionally wetting her clothes and undoing the buttons. She'd undo a button for a moment and then button it back up, and then she rolled up her skirt, exposing her smooth thighs, white and faintly red, which then spread to his ears and pimples and beat at his dismal defences.

Then she'd slam the window shut, crushing his desire and setting him pacing, carving grooves of turmoil into the mud roof. He was lost in a whirlwind of fear and angst, but he gathered all his strength and the lover-boy finally decided that all those weeks of excruciating torment were enough to make him knock at her door that evening.

He looked pitiful: he'd squeezed himself into his younger brother's blue trousers and was wearing the shirt his cousin had bought at the second-hand clothes' market, reeking of half a bottle's worth of cheap aftershave, his Brilliantine-drenched hair looking shiny and comical, and his pimples all the more hideous for his pathetic attempts to pop them and then being smothered with Ideal spot cream. She towered over him lithely, casting an ethereal glow all around him. Everything he'd practised before coming over, evaporated in an instant, and all he could say was, 'Can I have some water?' It took a superhuman effort for him to add, 'cold water.'

'But of course.' Her magic voice tugged at his blood cells, mesmerising him. She turned and walked into the house, swaying, and the rooftop Romeo beat his ingenious retreat. Still there was no escaping the bonds of her seduction. He stayed up that whole autumn night looking through her open window as she let her hair down, spilling over her body in the greenish light. She massaged her breasts with wood-sorrel flowers and the shoots of other

SARMADA

strange plants. She rubbed chamomiles under her arms and wild tulips and shy mint against her ivory breasts smeared lushly green. He came down from the roof like a sleepwalker and followed solace's path toward his destiny.

The door was half-open and two arms were waiting to grab him. Fingers as soft as bread-dough tickled the threshing-floor of his abdomen and wandered – herd-like – over the wilderness of his body. The fingers became stallions as they gripped his erection and changed his world forever. She squeezed him tightly as he fell to pieces in her hands. She saw his shirt-button and without thinking tore it off with her gleaming white teeth, then she stripped off all his clothes and laid him down on his back. Her mouth moistened the straw of his innocence as the bee of his body began to dance. He was at the point of bursting as she lowered herself onto his erection after licking the signpost of his body and before it had hardly taken shelter inside of her, it frothed and foamed, ejaculating in irregular spurts and then dying out. He swarmed as if a whole colony of bees were stinging his very blood, and then shrank inside of her as if turning to nothing. His blackness slipping out from her tenderness.

Her hands reached out, pulling him out of his pleasure coma and making him a man in a matter of minutes. A half hour later, she shuffled him out of the shed and he was alone once again. He cried for his loneliness, wiped out from exhaustion and mad delight, wondering what had just happened. He wanted to crawl back into her arms, to get back the innocence she'd shattered with her seduction. He wanted to get back the button she'd ripped off his shirt, but she'd locked the door and her body. Her rule was unshakable once he'd stepped out of the house: all the Sarmadan teenagers who attained their manhood in her shed on the surface of her intoxicating body had one chance and that was all.

One after the other, they came to see Farida and she marked them with her scent and tore a button from each of their shirts. She

86

took their gifts coolly and gave them a never-ending list of chores: they built a wall around the house, tiled the roof, installed running water, built a chicken-coop, painted the fence and the bars on the window. They performed tireless services – in secret, at first – and then openly with a good deal of pride and rivalry. Eventually it became something natural about the place. Her house was just like the majlis, or the church or the mosque: a place where people worshipped a lord who knew – better than anyone else – that everything was pre-determined.

She was accepted for what she was. Sarmada could deal with her captivating presence as she transformed the teenagers from permanent pains-in-the-arse to a troupe of gallant, light-footed poets. She acquired a strange kind of power over all the hormonal youths: she knew how to talk to them, how to advise them, how to listen to their souls and lift their spirits. They all obeyed the strict rule: no one could have her body more than once. She took a button from each one and showed him the door, sitting down straight after he'd left to sew the button onto a large white veil and she'd come up with a name or nickname for him, which she embroidered right there under his button, before going off to bathe her body – devoted to giving, not getting – in rose-perfumed water.

꿏

Yet she still waited for Shafee Mansour, the only one she herself longed for. She saw him, hanging around outside the house, monitoring her every move, counting her lovers, never capable of walking in himself. One evening after midnight, she caught him lurking in the garden, but when she whispered to him, 'Shafee, come in, don't be scared', he turned and ran.

She started arranging her days according to his schedule. He'd come in the morning and wait for her to open the door, then she would just look at him until she'd got her fill. She felt as if her day only started when she got to see him and then he would go off to join in the endless work dreamt up by Nawwaf to keep himself and all the other brothers busy, struggling to forget spilt blood through hard labour. When they'd finished their stone-hoeing, they began tilling and seeding, digging irrigation canals and planting trees, building walls, chopping firewood, working constantly to exhaust their guilt and shame. For her part, Farida received patients and prepared the requested cures: for stomach ills and indigestion, for high blood pressure, for increased fertility, tighter vaginas and whiter teeth. In the daytime, the eager teenagers came over to help out and by the afternoon, she'd decided which lucky boy would be next. That routine sometimes lasted for a month or more depending on her mood and the state of her garden.

'Shafee Mansour isn't like the rest,' she whispered over and over to herself. Shafee had those strangely sparkling sad eyes. He bore a too-heavy burden: he'd stabbed his own sister in front of the entire village and he'd never be able to shed the guilt or remorse. He was totally in thrall to his eldest brother Nawwaf's authority and to his own contradictory emotions – he didn't know whether to take refuge in God and wipe clean his guilt after shame had stained his family or to go to that abundantly feminine woman in the embroidered dress and dive into her curves until he drowned, or to wipe away the stench of blood that still lingered in his nose.

He hadn't slept since he first saw her, when she came to invite them around to her house for rice pudding. He tried with all his strength to drive her from his mind, but it was no use. He started going to her house every morning to wait for her to wake up so he could catch a glance that calmed his anxious soul. It was true that they'd been spared the crying plague – except for upset stomachs – even though they'd eaten the sweets the children had brought over, but ever since that day Shafee had been unable to sleep. Not because of the sweets, but more likely because of the pain that stabbed in his heart whenever he recalled her eyes and gentle voice. He returned in the evenings to pace back and forth, to catch a glance or a wave, and when she smiled his body ached, but the longing of his soul was eased. Nawwaf could see the signs on his youngest brother's face and he was struck by an old terror: he saw the same pallid confusion, the same moony insomnia he'd seen with Hela. If only he'd understood those signs when he'd first seen them, he'd have locked her up in the house or chased her lover out of town and saved his family the exile of spilt blood. He was worried about his youngest brother and every time he looked into his sweet, almost girlish face, he could see Hela.

On a bitter cold night in early 1970, with an icy wind whipping through Sarmada, Nawwaf walked in from the sitting room, wrapped in a thick fur and he could hear his brother crying in his bedroom. It was love and he knew it. He burst into the room, cursing and grabbing Shafee by the neck, lifting him off his feet as if he were a down pillow. He stared into his eyes and barked, 'Who is she? I'm not joking around: tell me who she is!'

Shafee was gasping for air, trying desperately to reach the ground with his feet. 'It's Farida, Nawwaf. Farida.' Nawwaf choked on the shock and dropped his brother onto the bed. He was livid; he stormed out into the cold, his breath melting the snow and rolled a cigarette. He inhaled the hot smoke voraciously until the cigarette burnt all the way down and singed his fingers. He went back inside the house like a raging, bellowing bull, threw on his heavy coat and grabbed his shotgun. He threw open the door and saw Shafee looking wasted like a misshapened down pillow.

'Get up, you son of a bitch. Get up and get dressed.'

Shafee obeyed as if hypnotised and his brother grabbed him by the hand and dragged him over to her house. He rapped at the door with the stock of his shotgun followed by incessant knocking from his massive hand. He could hear a voice on the inside, trembling, cold and scared: 'Who is it?'

'Open up, Farida.'

'Who's there?'

'Open up before I break down the door.'

'Give me a second.' She put on a heavy robe and grabbed the kerosene lamp before she opened the door.

Shafee was still a bit shell-shocked, chattering in the cold, and Nawwaf with his steaming breath looked rather like a snorting bull in the pale light of the lamp. He didn't want to drag it out so he simply threw his brother at her. 'Here, you whore! You can have him.' And then vanished into the icy darkness.

Back at the Mansour family home, Nayef, Talal and Shahir were sitting there worrying, wondering where their brothers had disappeared to in the cold. Nawwaf came back alone and threw a couple of cowchips into the stove and lit a fire. He sat there staring into space and none of his brothers dared to speak to him, or even go near his silence, booby-trapped as it was with mines that the slightest whisper would set off.

They all sat there together silently, and when the wood began to glow red, Nawwaf stood up and took the hot coals out with a pair of tongs and set the blackened teapot down on top of them, before adding three more cowchips and some oak logs to the stove. 'As soon as it gets to be the tail end of winter, we've got to move back to the old house. I think it's been long enough.' He sounded as if he'd walked in from another world, calm and resigned. Nayef and Talal nodded, but Shahir still couldn't shake his agonising foreboding and he blurted out – just as a log was popping in the fire:

'Where's Shafee?'

Nawwaf rolled a cigarette and took a deep drag. 'At Farida's.'

Nayef was shocked into silence, but Talal jumped out of his seat:

'For God's sake! Why didn't you bring him home? Why didn't you just shoot him on the spot? Oh, that dirty little son of a bitch!'

'Hela's blood wasn't enough, *Shaykhs*? You want us to kill him, too?' he asked his enraged brothers. 'I took him over there myself', he said defiantly.

At dawn, Talal and Nayef walked out of the parlour, packed their bags, hugged Shahir wordlessly, and then left for Khalwat al-Bayada on Mount Lebanon. They were never heard from again.

After Hela's death, the brothers had found themselves condemned to remain unseen, so they became Nawwaf's shadow, and when they walked anywhere together, they stepped silently, matching his footsteps. Talal and Nayef then had decided to become pious shaykhs, with white cowls, thick moustaches and shaved heads, dedicating their lives to copying out manuscripts of the Epistles of Wisdom. But they still remained dedicated to their older brother; he was the one who decided which direction all their lives would take. It was a kind of strange submission that could've lasted forever if Nawwaf hadn't done what he'd done. They couldn't understand why. How could a family, who'd paid such a high price for dignity with their own blood, sit idly by as their eldest brother lost all reason and himself delivered their youngest brother into the embrace of licentiousness? It was too much for Talal and Nayef to understand and their consent would have meant that their five and a half years of ostracism had just been a big joke. Their bold objection wasn't meant to insult their brother – whom they revered – and that was why they felt that all they could do was to go to the only place left where the saveable could be saved.

Shafee stayed at Farida's for two straight days. He was nearly dead from desperation, torment and the cold when his brother abandoned him to this love-loaded woman. She took him into the warmth of her bed and held him until the morning. He slept deeply in her arms and she chose not to wake him. She left him in bed and heated up the place. Then she brought him breakfast, not letting him get out of bed, and fed him – over his objections – a boiled egg dipped in ghee and made him drink a glass of milk. She didn't add any drops of grief-milk to it because she wanted him exactly as he was, under no influences at all; she wanted his tender heart, his unexaggerated soul, and she understood why she was so drawn to him.

He ate and smiled, and then he fell back asleep. He slept all day as she took care of her business and received customers wanting her herbs. She took care of all their orders and then she returned to him. She watched his face in the light of the paraffin lamp and saw that the drowsy clouds had all cleared away. She stood there, not knowing what to do, and for the first time, she was truly frightened: this boy's going to stay here! She'd never let any of her lovers stay the night before.

She wanted nothing more than for this overwhelming affection she felt for him to be transformed into mere desire, and yet she felt as if every fibre of her body craved him. She kept her nightgown on and slipped into bed beside him. He moved closer to kiss her, but she jerked her lips away; she didn't want anything resembling love to intrude on this night. She feared the torment of an infatuated heart and kisses were the shocking, painful gateway to a land of simultaneous joy and hurt called love. She didn't want to fall for him, to love him, for it could never be undone.

He kissed her slender neck, whispering breathily, and she could only surrender. She usually had to guide her body-tormented teenage lovers, who'd yet to learn the secrets of vague desires and still hadn't learnt the difference between maternal and sexual passion and love, but he, she felt, was complete. He smelt unlike any other man she knew. His body was supple and strong: subtly sculpted, she felt as she ran her hands over his tight muscles. That's why she let him kiss her neck, and nibble her earlobes, and take off her nightgown, leaving her naked. That's why she let him celebrate every inch of her skin with his hot tongue, and suck her breasts – not ferociously, but gently, exciting her desire. He squeezed her breasts together and slipped both nipples into his mouth at once, sucking hard and biting, but stopping just before it hurt, and pulling away and blowing coolly as his saliva seeped into her skin. He continued down, licking at her belly and then his tongue came into contact with her invisible, almost microscopic, pubic hair, causing it to stand on end. It sent mysterious signals to her brain telling it to transmit quivering waves all over her body. He travelled down between her thighs, kissing her, smelling her, rubbing his face against her, and then he rested his chin against her pubis.

He was led by instinct and hunger. Her amulet's riddle deciphered, he brought his face back up to her pelvis, lapping at her, dipping his tongue inside of her, teasing her clitoris, rubbing his nose against the secret spot none of her young men had discovered. She was wet, she was fragrant, and she writhed. And then she came, for the first time in her entire life. He slid down to her feet, sucking each of her toes and licking her heels and calves. He was completely absorbed in discovering every spot on her body, its hidden secrets, and he was in no hurry for it to end. He wanted to go over – and down into – her every pore.

She was light in his arms as he manoeuvred her into any position he felt like, but his erection was like stone as she reached out to grasp it. It wasn't overly large or unsuitably small.

She swooned as she knelt down in front of him, feeling his veins, holding his penis back as she ran her tongue down over his testicles and took them in her mouth. She dipped them in and out, and then she pushed him down onto his back and knelt over him like a cupola, staring at him with brassy eyes, and then she resumed her tonguing, sliding down his chest to his stomach and coming to his erection, licking the engorged head, and bringing it into her mouth. Shivers rippled through his entire body as she removed it slowly and held it, like a fluttering, placing light kisses on his jumpy veins, and then taking it back into her mouth. She swallowed it down until she could feel his pubic hair against her lips. She wanted to give him what she'd been unable to give anyone else.

He entered her, lowering himself down on top of her as he looked into her eyes, glazed over with pleasure and fear. Then before she could say anything, he put her on all fours and entered her from behind. She didn't know how many times she'd come, but when he pulled out of her, she felt like her soul was slipping away. He suddenly forced it into her arse, ignoring her pleas. 'Stop! You're hurting me! Please stop!'

He could hear nothing over his own exhilaration as he rode

her – in and out; it burnt her insides. He moved back and forth between her vagina and arse, as he repeated, 'Farida, you slut. Farida, you bitch. You whore.' She caught a lusty fever from those words and she seemed to glow with pleasure. Her body, she felt, was finally being liberated from the worship of those teenagers who sanctified its motherly affection. The repugnant words set her free and added to her ecstasy. She longed to hear more and more; she wanted his force to blow her body up. Remembering the naïve, empty words of love on teenagers' whispering lips, she felt her femininity was being washed clean of all that had clung to it. She felt the membrane of her innocence sloughing off the dust of desperate love. He was giving her everything he had stored up in his dictionary of filth without embellishment or emotion; taking the body to this lit-up point as every atom burst open and was soaked with sweat and exhaled pleasure. The trembling never ceased. She reached peaks she'd never known. Images ruptured in her mind as it clung to extreme heights. She felt her soul dissolving; her body disintegrating, mixing with spheres of light, spurting, sea-foaming, overflowing with heat. Until it came time for him to come and he let loose a round of semen on her back and then grabbed himself tightly, squeezing it, biting down on his lip till it bled, and frantically lay her back down in her crib and yanking at her head to slip his flushed member between her lips before it exploded in her mouth.

Shafee was all hysterical giggling and filthy slurs as she swallowed his milk and nursed him until gradually it withered. Only the erring, heart-twisting words her lover repeated could bring her back to reality: 'Oh, Hela … Hela … You're such a slut, Hela.'

He returned to his brothers the next day, exhausted but full. His face was white and bright, but clearly hiding something. There was a striking glimmer in his eyes that burnt out as soon as he found out that two of his brothers had left and that Nawwaf was refusing to speak to him. His other brother Shahir simply slapped him and spit in his face. He wiped his face calmly and went to wash.

He came out to see Nawwaf and Shahir packing up whatever they could, getting ready to move back into the old house. He worked alongside them in silence; he was energetic and active. He went over to the old house and cleaned the place and tidied up. He threw himself into work like a madman, and every time his memory threw up a scene from what had happened at Farida's, his energy increased, gaily in his body, shining out of his eyes, in a way that was obvious to everyone. His brothers were shocked to find that the old run-down house had come back to life and that they could move back in that very evening. What made it even more poignant was that their youngest brother had a child-like smile on his face, which made them smile in turn, before they remembered themselves and stared down at the ground, erasing any trace of smiles, putting on masks of threadbare anger.

He was dying to get back to Farida, but he was blocked by the gaze of his brothers who never ceased heaping blame on him, which he couldn't bear.

A week after the remaining brothers returned to the house, they invited the notables of Sarmada to a reception that would allow them to rejoin the life of the community. They slaughtered seven sheep and prepared twenty-one trays of mansaf, and then they slaughtered another seven sheep and distributed the meat among the poor. Everyone accepted their decision and the hospitality they were known for.

Shafee was watching her through the bushes, so she hid quickly. She started trying to avoid him. She was enforcing her rule – one time only, that was all, just like anybody else – but it pained her, too, not to have him.

She worried that love would lead them down a path from which there was no turning back and that he would consume her soul and the opening up of her body. When he said Hela's name, she was brought back to reality and she knew for certain, and sadly, that she couldn't love a damaged, pained adolescent who was condemned by himself and God and society to an eternal punishment because he murdered his innocent sister on delusional grounds known as 'honour'. She refused all his winning attempts to see her and burned her memories down to ash so that it was as if nothing at all had ever happened between them.

It went on like that for weeks and then he made up his mind. He wrapped his gift in a bag and knocked on her door. She knew it was him, so she didn't open the door. He knew she wouldn't open up, but he wanted to settle his doubts so he could carry out what he'd decided to do; he knocked again and again, and again. Then he called to her through the door: 'I'm leaving something for you here by the door. I just wanted to tell you that I'm leaving for good, but that I'll never forget you.'

He walked away from the house and hid behind the big cactus near the entrance. She opened the door a few minutes later and took the package inside. She looked into the void, but she didn't see him. She stared into the void; she could feel him nearby. She waved. It was the last time he'd ever lay eyes on her. The next morning he set out for Beirut, where he waited for the ship that would take him to Colombia never to be heard from again.

She opened the bag and found a transistor radio that he'd ordered especially for her. The brown radio was about as big as a tray of tomatoes and it would fill her life with news and songs until the very end. It was on the radio that she learnt that there'd been a Corrective Revolution and that a new future awaited Syria. She didn't understand a word of it, but she started noticing as her adolescent lovers began parroting strange new words about liberty, unity and socialism – all the brand-new Baath party slogans.

Yet there wasn't a force on earth that could alter the routine she'd established. She was like Sarmada: whatever was going on in the world marched along easily until it got to this volcanic plain where its seeds might be accepted, but its roots always failed to penetrate the ground. Four houses down, the remaining members of the Mansour family were working to win back their family's

good name. Nawwaf didn't seem to care and he told his brother
that he wanted to marry him off.

'Not right now, brother,' Shahir answered calmly.

ৡ

Several defiant years later, dozens and dozens of teenage boys
had passed through her house, but now she was showing signs
of pregnancy; she could feel it growing inside of her. Despite all
her careful precautions, pregnancy surprised her with a reality she
could clearly see.

Every time she considered killing her foetus, she knew she
wouldn't be able to forgive herself if she did. She also knew that
accepting a fatherless child was too much to ask of Sarmada's abili-
ties and sensibilities; it was impossible for a bastard to get along
in a place so tied to its rigid rules. Thus she decided she'd choose
a husband who wouldn't interfere with what she considered to be
her divine mission. When one of her teenage lovers was talking
to her about the mission of the Arab nation and its renaissance,
she cut off his nonsense and said, 'I've got a mission to do, too,'
and kicked him out of the house to spread news of the miraculous
body and its revelation.

Long story short, she thought it over and decided there was no
one better for her than Hamoud, the crackpot.

By the tenth of June 1967 it was clear that the defeat was total.
The loss of Quneitra and the Golan Heights combined with the
occupation of Sinai, Jerusalem and the West Bank – a defeat
on that scale – was too much for the geography teacher, who'd
believed all his government's lies. He didn't sleep at all on the sixth
night; he stayed up listening to the radio and when he heard the
announcement that Quneitra had fallen he guzzled down half a
bottle of straight arak. When he returned home from the local
party meeting, boiling with rage against the enemies of Arab

nationalism, he tried to turn his wife's body into the Arab nation. He stripped off her clothes and got started – no time to lose! He plotted a grid over her entire body with a black marker and began sketching a map.

At first, she thought it was just a fit of his uniquely mad lust, which she'd always enjoyed, for he never stopped thinking up new ways to measure and sketch maps of pleasure over her body's secret terrain, but then he just kept on sketching maps of the Arab world. He was convinced that the solution to the world's problems lay in maps, which never lied, and that everyone should just keep to their borders and discover the treasures they possessed.

On that day, he transmigrated the souls of Sykes and Picot as he divided up the parts of his wife Ibtihal's body up into the territory of the former colonial powers. When he came to her vagina, he drew Palestine and looked at her as he shouted, completely naked himself, 'You tricked us, you sons of bitches! You gave us everything and you took away the womb!' As he gripped the scalpel in his hand, he knew he wanted to kill international Zionism and a terrified Ibtihal got up and ran into the bathroom and locked the door, and when he finally passed out on the bed from the defeat and his drunkenness, she ran away to her family in the north and never returned.

Hamoud lost half his mind after the defeat in the June War and the Party found they no longer required his services. He spent his days, shouting at the village: 'Shut your doors! Don't leave anything unlocked. Shut your doors!' He wouldn't go to sleep until he'd gone around to every house in the village and made sure the doors were locked. Nothing made him angrier than an unlocked door someone had forgotten about. Unlocked doors reminded Hamoud, the brilliant geography teacher and committed Baathist, of the night Ibtihal ran away.

It wasn't his geographic lust that'd scared her off, it was more likely that she'd just been waiting for the chance to get back at him for the awful poverty he'd put her through since he was a member of the Baath who donated his salary to his brother-Arabs from the Gulf to the Atlantic. He memorised the party's theoretical principles as if they were the names of God. He was overflowing with a fervour that could accept no alternative to the ineluctable destiny of liberty, unity and socialism. He'd wanted Ibtihal to be his wholly committed, freedom-fighting comrade-partner and to discipline herself strictly for the sake of the cause of the Great Arab Revolution to come, but the aftermath of the June defeat was too much for his mind to handle – loaded as it was with thoughts of coming revolutions.

After going around to all the doors and making sure they were locked, he'd head off to bed and in the mornings, he'd get up bright and early to take care of the holy chores that Mother Nature cryptically sent to him. He shaved, washed in cold water – in summer or winter, it didn't matter – shined his shoes, put on cologne, gathered up his maps and great secrets, along with a big compass, protractor and astrolabe, and set off for Wind Hill. There, he measured God's country and noted the signs until he reached the Salt Spring. He would sit there in the stream, lost in thought, announcing his peculiar daily prophecies, synthesising signs and symbols, reading faint clues, jotting down his amazing five-line poems in a big book he called *Uncovering Falsehood*. He erased whatever he'd written every night before he went to bed so that the hidden evil forces wouldn't get hold of his secrets.

He knew when solar and lunar eclipses would take place, he was an excellent geomancer, and he spent most of his time doing complex calculations to determine precisely at what time God would wake up. 'Our lives are a divine dream,' he'd say. 'Everything that happens is a dream. And God's dreams only last three minutes. Every second is a million years so it's not over yet. One day he's going to wake up and then everything will go back to how it started.'

He carried a book with him wrapped in the eighth of March 1963 issue of the Baathist newspaper *Militant*; this was the day when the Baathists triumphed over the Separatists to rule Syria for an endless forever. For decades long it seemed entrenched and unshakable, but places have their own logic and maybe all it takes is one distant spark to burn the whole thing down. Sarmada got used to him and it wasn't as if he went around poking his nose into other people's business – aside from the doors, of course.

His garden was turned into a lab where he built his ridiculous time machines out of crates and cardboard and junk. His furniture was draped with dozens of maps that showed what lay beyond geography itself. 'Everything has a unit of measurement,' he said. 'Everything has a map, from galaxies to atoms. Anything that doesn't get a map is worthless.'

Over time, they discovered he had lots of amazing talents, and while it was true that the name 'Hamoud, the crackpot' had stuck, it was born out of the villagers' sympathy and their lingering respect for a man who was naturally both noble and crazy.

Farida knew just how to lure him in. She'd known ever since he started coming round to her shed to make sure the door was locked. The next evening after she'd decided that Hamoud the crackpot was the man for her – the man who could give the foetus forming inside of her a chance at life – she tied the door with a rope to keep it open and waited for him to come. She put on a thin slip so that the features of her body could draw in the topographically-obsessed geography teacher, and she perfumed the house with very rare incense she'd been given by one of her teenagers who'd left with his family for Saudi Arabia. The boy had stolen some outstanding Cambodian incense and presented it to the woman who'd given meaning to his adolescence. She burnt the incense with some fragrant resin, turning the whole atmosphere of the house into one of seduction, and she added some of her own homemade incense, which gave off scents mixed with magic that couldn't be compared to moments of basil, whispers of mischievous jasmine, or the rapture of wily damask rose. It was as if the scents were a language that could communicate directly with Hamoud's mind when he did indeed turn up, as he did most days after sunset. He grabbed the roped door and yanked it angrily, but there was no use. He tried again with some force, but again he failed. She stepped out from between the ferns of green-tinged seconds, her perky breasts barely hidden by her lace slip, her alluring curls bouncing and flashing as they fell over her shoulders, her long neck and big eyes protected by arched, heart-snaring eyebrows. She called to him, parting those cherry-red lips overlaid with crimson-lipstick, and her straight, white teeth, made him freeze stock-still in the face of this oncoming army.

His agitation-aching head was begging him to run, but some hidden desire and his geographic curiosity ordered him to stay and wait to see this convoy and the strange storm of scents it brought with it up close. Before he could even make up his mind, her perfume of incense, orange-blossom water and other essences, and the spices wafting from her body, caused a little – maybe too little to see even – drool to form at the corner of his gaping mouth.

'Having trouble?' Her question knocked him down and it was followed by the sweeping convoy of her body, every last detail of which was bewitchingly revealed.

She bent down over the knot on the door handle, three-quarters of her chest spilling out, and the totally defeated teacher's jaw dropped to the floor. She untied the knot easily and they both – the door and the teacher – jerked. She calmly shut the door, slid the bolt to lock it, and unlocked the gates to a geography the teacher had never known before.

She took him by the hand and sat him down on the sofa. She knelt down in front of him and took off his gleaming shoes and bright-white socks. She undid his belt and took off his trousers, and when he saw she'd folded them carefully, he thanked her from the bottom of his heart. She stripped him down completely and took him over to her washbasin, which was really just a barrel she'd cut in half, length-wise, herself. She poured water all over him and sat him down in the water on the surface of which floated troops of rascally camomile, red poppy anemone, and clover flowers, and she began to scoop up the water embroidered with the conspiratorial flowers into a plastic bowl and pour them over his head, filled with Baath party slogans and doctrines. This was followed by a ritual massage of his stiff shoulders that made the hairs on his shoulders stick up and she continued lavishing him with her abundant affection, massaging his muscles, which had ached for a touch like that. She took him out of the pond of sweetness and laid him on his back in the bed of wonder. She blindfolded him with a silk scarf, but despite the overwhelming darkness, the lamp of his body lit up his docile vision, and he gave into her entirely as she massaged him with sesame oil that she'd pressed herself from seeds she'd carefully selected, and then distilled the oil with a chemist's care, using all her talent and experience. It made his desiccated body spring to life. It shook its every hungry cell, and he was overcome by a current that shocked all his muscles and then they relaxed, and for the first time since Ibtihal had left, his erection sprung up. She fed him one of her grief milk soaked sweets, which he followed with a swig of wine she'd aged in casks. He could smell the hillside grapevines bathing in the drowsy sunlight, washed in clean breezes. The scent of the wine mixed with the scent of her body made it the best wine in the entire world. Ever since the days when the mountains produced an emperor of Rome, Philip the Arab, Rome had drunk the wine of Sarmada and the surrounding regions. He could almost hear nature trotting and history shouting as they slid over his tongue and down into his bitter-filled throat. He finished his glass, so she laid down beside him, burying his face, tanned with repressed anger, in her breasts. He began to suck on them and then to sob. He spent the first half of that moonlit night in tears. She was soaked by his irrepressible tears, which streamed out from his heavy gloom. When he was finally freed from the sorrow-showers of his bitter memories: from the ungrateful abandonment of a party he'd given his life to and a woman he'd been devoted to, he was overcome by a forceful desire as she rode him with all her femininity. As he erupted into her womb, he cried out, 'I am al-Idrisi! I am al-Idrisi!'

She got off him and lay down beside him, kissing his overgrown, polo-stick-shaped ear lobes, and whispered to him – not to be nosy, but just to ask: 'Who's al-Idrisi?'

'The author of *The Book of Wonders for those with Lust to Wander.*'

He stood up, striking a teacher's pose and she sat down on the floor leaning forward onto the sofa, drinking her wine, and listening to him as she smiled.

'He was the first person to draw maps, unlock the secret symbols of the land and paint the seas; he drew connections between human life and the environment. Al-Idrisi was born in Ceuta and lived in Cordoba. He travelled to Syria to study and then he went to Norman Sicily to draw the first map that represented the world, or close to it. One second', he said, reaching for his bag. He pulled out a stack of maps and carefully picked one of them: 'Look at this map here. It's an exact copy of al-Idrisi's. Look how he drew the seven climes with all the countries and continents and the distances between countries, the routes and the mileage. His books on geography are a highpoint in Arab geographical texts, and in all of medieval science.

'Al-Idrisi died at the age of seventy-one but no one knows where he was buried. I think he died while he was still at the Norman court in Palermo, Sicily.'

He continued demonstrating his wide knowledge as she watched this amazing man, sometimes holding back her laughter and at other times with her mouth gaping in wonder.

'Al-Idrisi was followed by Yaqut al-Hamawi and al-Istakhri and Ibn Battuta and Ibn Majid al-Maqdisi; they all knew the earth was round before everyone else. They understood about lunar and solar eclipses and seasons and the earth's rotation and its orbit around the sun, with their eyes, their minds and their tools, which I have with me in my bag.'

He was full of information and explanations. Farida was visited by every Arab geographer and explorer in an amazing exposition until Hamoud passed out. He woke up at noon the next day to the smell of frying eggs; he had a slight headache and his madness seemed to have disappeared.

'Where's Ibtihal?' he asked her with evident shyness.

'She died years ago,' she said firmly. 'Come on now, no time to waste, breakfast's ready.' She brought over a tray festooned with cheese, yogurt, milk, honey, stuffed eggplant, radishes and eggs sunny-side-up, as he tried to remember what had happened the night before. All he could remember was that it was day eight of the war! That the soldiers who passed by Sarmada had been shouting: 'They wouldn't have occupied it if it weren't for the announcement that Quneitra had fallen! We retreated haphazardly. They tricked us! The Israelis are cowards; they wouldn't have been able to move up if they hadn't announced the fall of Quneitra.'

He remembered that he'd drunk half a litre of homemade arak and that he'd been drunk up until this moment. Five years had passed since the defeat and he'd been lost in his own world. He'd only just snapped out of it, smelling the remnants of the incense, and oil and perfume. They lingered there in his nose.

'I slept for a long time, didn't I?' he asked her.

'Not really. Only for four or five years,' she said, laughing gaily. 'Come on, let's eat and then we can go register our marriage.'

He thought for a moment: 'Whatever you say.'

She let out a deep sigh, from the worry and fear that had been plaguing her, as Hamoud ate silently. He caught sight of the compass leaning against the bolted door. That's strange, he thought. What's that doing here?

Chapter Three

Buthayna

Should I call it quits and go? It was the hope of escape that had me standing on the roof, surveying the whole of Sarmada. What was waiting there in that silent, stoic village? What was coalescing beneath its stones and bricks and in the torment of its people? Anyone who watched the sun set during that fiery summer would feel a great womb contracting, getting ready to give birth to new creatures and lineages the earth had never seen before. You could tell it was on the verge of erupting. The Hauran Plain and its spirits were reflected in the remnants of dried-out plants and harvested fields, yellow as if sickly, stretching across the surface of this poor, confused, forgotten place in the south. Here, power lies exclusively in the dried-up brush and chaff and all it takes is one match to set everything alight. Fire consumes everything; it consumes every last stockpiled drop of water on this earth. And all it takes is one breeze to make dust the ruler of the place. Dust covers faces, despair shows in their eyes, and the people are slaves to the most acute thoughtlessness.

One spark is enough to revive their desire for life. One clue from the place is all it would take to change things forever. Silent labour pains echo through the place, summoning up blood, and souls, and stones.

I couldn't go back to the way I'd been, but I couldn't go forward either. I was stuck between two worlds, two moments, two histories.

The East that had produced three faiths was getting ready to produce a fourth and this time it was going to be a different type of energy that would overwhelm the entire world. A world that would resemble itself and wouldn't stem from any one person. After we'd convinced ourselves that the earth was round, it was inevitable that we'd put up with anything, and thus we could no longer pretend to kick the bad apples off into the abyss.

Sarmada's the centre of the world tonight, so, of course, I'm going to stay an extra day and listen.

I wrote those words in my notebook and walked back down, having had my fill of the Hauran sunset.

Sarmada had many names: 'Mother of Trees', 'Windhill', 'God's Basin', and all these names reflected the nature of the place and the character of its people: so modest they were naïve, so excitable they were rash, so profound they knew all the different ways one could be God-fearing.

It was also the setting for many jokes and anecdotes, most of which stemmed from the village's ancient trade in cannabis before it was outlawed. They used to grow it in the fields, process it and dry it in their houses. It made the best hashish in the East, which they used to export to Beirut and Jerusalem. During the hashish harvest, the village was drowned in good spirits and constant laughter, not scowling like all the villages around it. Men and women, the young and the elderly, everyone took part in the hashish harvest and it was like a festival. After the authorities cracked down, people lost the sense of humour they'd relied on to endure the passing of time.

It was an ordinary mountain village in the Hauran and to excavate its memories meant having to find a gap in the layers of time. There was never any logical explanation for what happened, and everything that happened seemed illogical. But the truth, which the eye couldn't deny – and you'll see it if any of you have the chance to go visit – was that it was stunningly green, surrounded by olive groves on three sides, while the western flank was given over to a plain open to all possibilities.

Growing hashish and getting high was something the villagers had always done and there was nothing that could stamp it out. In Sarmada, history had always stayed at the margins. They never got involved in it except when it was time for an armed revolution. They didn't have much patience for non-violent resistance – no matter how celebrated – they weren't good at inventing demands, or listening to reason, but when they rose up, when they felt their very existence was under threat, they were unstoppable; they tore down everything in sight. And yet they never learnt how to preserve the achievements of the revolutions they'd launched throughout history. The thing they really excelled at was biding their time.

They had the unshakable belief that their lives would be repeated, so there was no harm if one generation was lost. The thing about history though, was that it usually took a place a very long time to know itself before it submitted, so time simply won through attrition.

Sarmada was made of basalt, lately invaded by cement, and the valley, stretching down from the mountain peaks, split into two branches encircling and embracing the village as it continued on toward the Yarmouk Valley.

Windhill was like a pillow the village rested against. The families who lived there were Christians and Druze who'd come to the mountains from the Lebanon more than 300 years ago. Bedouins were settled around it in an attempt to put an end to their nomadic lifestyles.

The village was ringed by groves of olive and fig trees and after the revolution when the decision was made to rip all the opium poppies out of the fields, the land was reclaimed for wheat, barley, grass peas, vetch and chickpeas encroaching into the Hauran Plain, and parts of the dark blue, rugged wasteland of basalt rock were also cultivated, so the village took on the appearance of a heap of life surrounded by a jungle of blue rock, tinged with black.

The legendary Mother of Rams tree stood right in the centre of the rocky wasteland, and there wasn't another green shoot within a ten-kilometre radius among the silent stones. The tree had become a place of pilgrimage for people longing to be fertile. They'd take the leaves and make a bitter tea out of them in the hope that it would bring their barren wombs to life. Sheep were slaughtered there and stories were woven around it, which all said that it was a blessed tree which fed on the blood of vigorous rams and would ensure the safety of a flock. The shepherds lavished the tree with their best rams whenever their flocks were attacked by wolves or other predators, or if a deadly disease struck.

The tree grew in a frightening and desolate rocky wasteland and it took its name from the offerings slaughtered over its roots. Over time it came to mark Sarmada's imaginary outer limits.

The second famous tree was the pleasure-laced terebinth tree that stood on the edge of the valley. Stone-deaf Siman had looked after it for twenty-five years. It was an ancient tree that time had forgotten: it had survived the great volcano, three earthquakes and more than thirty battles that had taken place nearby. The Turkish soldiers, who'd been tasked with getting firewood for the Hejaz railway trains and had cut down and torn up a third of the forest on the mountain, hadn't been able to cut it down. It was more than 4,000 years old and owing to its great age, it grew new trunks, which then grew old and died and were replaced by others. But the mother tree remained there fixed and towering, with its sticky, moist clefts.

The inside of the tree was moist and smooth and warm, and Stone-deaf Siman found it was a much nicer place to see to his needs compared to the usual taking of matters into one's own hands. Then it occurred to him that he might profit from the tree. He built a brick wall around the tree and hung up a curtain of hessian sacks, and he himself became the tree's official pimp! He was the one who found the customers, and looked after it, and pruned it.

The third famous tree in Sarmada stood in front of Mamdouh's shop. It was more than a hundred years old – a giant white poplar tree that stretched up far above the houses and became the preferred resting spot of all the transitory and local birds. On pleasant evenings, the bird chorus could be heard outside Sarmada, splitting apart, intertwining, a floating jungle expertly arranged by the birds themselves. Mamdouh the shopkeeper was worried that the tree's massive roots would destroy the foundation of his house so, three ruined chainsaws and four days of backbreaking labour later, he managed to cut it down. Every evening for weeks the sparrows of Sarmada would circle the void, their chirping choked, and many of them found they couldn't sleep in any other tree.

As flocks of sparrows circled in the emptiness, frantically searching for their uprooted home and not comprehending how such a huge green tree could suddenly disappear, they began to spray their shit on the village below. They cheeped angrily in the sky above Sarmada for three whole days as Farida, stuck somewhere between life and death, gave birth to her child – her screams breaking through the lost sparrows' cries.

Hamoud stood on the roof of the shed, performing the ancient custom: whenever there was a difficult birth, the husband would jump up and down on the roof over the room where his wife lay to help with the birth of the baby. For three days, Hamoud danced a manic Dabke on the roof, covered in birdshit and people's scorn, but the child was finally born and when he heard its cry and the midwife and neighbour women ululating in celebration, he came running down like a crazy man, jostling at the door, and then running over to the shop to buy walnuts and sweets for the happy occasion. The women inside the shed began muttering the name of God. The newborn boy had two pieces of flesh between his thighs. Umm Dhiyab washed the baby and swaddled him carefully before handing him to his mother. 'Is it a boy or a girl?' asked an exhausted Farida.

'A boy and more,' answered the midwife. 'He's got two! Praise the Lord.'

'I'm going to call him Bulkhayr,' said Farida. 'His name's Bulkhayr.

Farida's shed saw two months of busy celebration and a pungent tea of boiled herbs was distributed to the people of Sarmada. The indomitably proud father carried his little boy against his chest and stayed up all night looking after him. He changed his nappy and cradled him. He told him stories about the great Arab explorers. He rubbed him down with olive oil and massaged his tender limbs. He did everything carefully and on time, and with a touching affection as if he'd lost all hope of ever having a child and then suddenly been surprised by fatherhood.

It was undeniable that ever since Farida and Hamoud had been married, she'd become a faithful wife and gave her husband all her loyalty and love, out of a combination of guilt and a longing for purification, that she lavished on him the abundance of her body and womanliness, that she'd shut and sealed once and for all the doors and windows of her past, but still she'd never expected that he'd treat her child with such love. When she finally decided to tell him the truth: that the child wasn't his, she found he already knew.

On the day she'd decided to apologise and to thank him, the October War broke out and brought Hamoud's erstwhile happiness back with it, so she decided never to bring it up again, especially when she saw him climb up to the roof, watching ecstatically as the Israeli Phantom jets burned up near Sarmada. He immediately enlisted in the army without a moment's thought and his enthusiasm took him all the way to the front line where he joined the fighting over two days until the Syrian army reached Lake Tiberias. After the ceasefire came into effect on the Egyptian front, he returned with his division and took part in the war of attrition over eighty-one days, only to disappear again. He was most likely taken prisoner. He still hadn't returned after the war was over. Some said he was dead for certain, while others who'd fought alongside him, said that he was part of a group who'd all been captured.

The people of Sarmada were busy mourning their martyr: Shahir Mansour was Sarmada's only fallen soldier. He was buried in an august ceremony that included a few eulogies and the people of Sarmada donated money to build a memorial for him at the entrance to the town before Poppy Bridge. The flag of Sarmada flew for the martyr that day for he was the son of the great revolutionary Hamad al-Mansour, one of the heroes of Syria's struggle against French occupation and the flag-bearer who'd distinguished himself for valour in the Battles at Kafr and Mazraa. The crowd was quiet and wondering – a certain lingering question made them uneasy. The Mansour family was the most freedom-loving and independent-minded family in the whole of the mountain region and they took pride in their long legacy of repelling anyone who came and tried to impose their will and laws on them. Their ancestor had refused every last Ottoman edict and his grandsons had fought against Ibrahim Pasha and twice decimated his army. The martyr's father had been a wanted fugitive until the French finally left Syria and his uncle had taken part in all the great uprisings, but then how could the heir of a family who considered freedom so sacred bring himself to kill his sister, who wanted only the same right to choose her own life partner and as a result was slaughtered like a lamb?

Two months had passed since the Mansour family's martyr was buried at Khashkhasha cemetery when Nawwaf went out of the parlour and let off a magazine of bullets to quiet the howling wolves. But when they went on howling even louder, he went up to the roof and started howling himself, imitating them, until the morning. After that he locked himself away at home, lost in other worlds, talking only to himself, and every time the moon was full and the sky was clear, he'd go up onto the roof of the house and begin to howl.

With the blooming of her motherhood and breast milk, Farida was struck by a creeping fear, a painful shame, which she quickly shook off. She'd made up her mind: she was going to purify herself of any remnants of her past life. She took her son to the village nurse, whom everyone called Doctor Salem, and he examined the two tender pieces of flesh between the little boy's thighs and discovered that they were connected at the base. After a few minutes, he turned to her and said, 'This is a blessing, not some kind of punishment. Don't you ever think of having one of them removed.'

She lived only for Bulkhayr and built her entire life around him. Her plants were no longer as lush as they'd once been, but the great joy she took in her baby caused her to withdraw from her cherished hobby. She decided it was enough just to have him circumcised like all the boys in Sarmada, whether Christian, Muslim or Druze.

One day when she went to get some of the grief-milk cheese out of the store, she saw it had been infiltrated by worms, so she threw the whole lot out and stopped making and selling her life-changing cheese and drinks mixed with the strange tasting milk.

She went to the Hamza Majlis and asked the shaykhs to be inducted into her religion. She was refused time and time again and she couldn't find two shaykhs to support her initiation. In order for her to become a Druze initiate, there was a ritual: two shaykhs – two men or women – who were already initiates themselves, had to sponsor her and take responsibility, in front of all the other shaykhs and God, that the inductee was pure of soul and that they had lived an unimpeachably moral life as required and that they were confident that the inductee would abandon all traces of a worldly life. Unlike all the other religions in the world, there was no proselytising. People were left to decide for themselves when it was the right time to come into the fold because if anyone went back on their initiation, it was considered final and their requests for initiation would never be honoured again. There was no set age for someone who wanted to be initiated into the religion and gain access to the six religious texts: as soon as a Druze man or woman had undergone puberty and was physically mature, they were eligible – those who wished – to enter the religion. There's no rule that you have to be forty before you can become an initiated Druze as the misinformed believe.

As for the people who didn't want to enter, they were never compelled or chastised, and they weren't even required to live by the religious laws. They were simply left to fill their own spiritual voids however they pleased.

After she'd tried and failed multiple times to be admitted to the religion, she headed to the church and met with Father Elias. She explained to him that she desperately needed God and that she was ready to accept her faith, but that the shaykhs wouldn't let her. She asked him for a favour and the graceful priest answered: 'I'll do anything in my power to help you, my child.'

'Do you think you could hear my confession? Maybe God will forgive me with your help.'

The priest laughed. 'But, Farida, you belong at the majlis. You're a Druze, my child.'

'Yes, Father, I know, but what's the difference between a majlis or a church or a mosque? Aren't they all houses of God? God love you, hear my confession and let me repent.'

Father Elias consented and took her over to the confessional. When they were finished, she asked him if he would baptise Bulkhayr and he agreed.

That evening, Father Elias went to see the head shaykh of Sarmada and broached the subject of Farida. 'Who's the father of her child?' asked Shaykh Farouq.

'He's from Sarmada, Shaykh,' said Father Elias. 'It's better if we preserve her privacy and just help her. God's mercy knows no bounds.' Shaykh Shaheen agreed to initiate Farida in her faith, but on one condition: that she remain on the periphery, which meant that she'd only be allowed to read the commentaries on the Epistles of Wisdom and not the Epistles themselves until the fitness of her soul could be confirmed and that when the shaykhs read from the essential texts of wisdom in the Majlis, she would have to step outside.

The sight of Bulkhayr's little moon-like face sent Farida into raptures of a mysterious, soul-tickling joy and she wanted nothing more than to be the sort of mother he could be proud of. She wore black in mourning for Hamoud, who'd disappeared into the fog of captivity or into an unknown and unverifiable death. Her life changed completely and became an unending stream of helping others and joining in their occasions, both happy and sad. Her healing herbs and potions were now accompanied by great gratitude. The total transformation in her life could hardly be compared to regret, which the men of the cloth would have preferred. 'She's still got that bold look in her eyes,' whispered Shaykh Farouq to Father Elias, meaning she hadn't been broken, hadn't been moved by the demanded apologies and self-reproach to plead intercession from God's vicars on earth.

Her shed, shrouded and burdened with all those secret teenage rendezvouses, threw open its doors to a new life. It had lost its former lustre, but cloaked itself in something new. Sarmada was, after all, open to certain changes: young people in the peaceful village who longed for change and were affected by everything that what was happening in Syria and the Middle East began to form cells. The farmers were surprised to find a bunch of communist youths volunteering to help them with the reaping and harvest. Those youths, with endless energy and enthusiasm for change, managed to win many farmers' hearts before the government set the Baathists on them and ruined their reputation by claiming that they were all godless infidels calling for sin and anarchy.

Farida was amazed by the transformation in the course of her powerful desires and the cold cloak that had fallen over her hot body like hibernation. The dominating desires lay dormant and little by little she was transformed into an incomparably loving and gentle, even somewhat imprudent, mother. Had they disappeared or merely paused? She didn't want to know. She was too busy celebrating her motherhood and she left life to take whatever path it chose.

She didn't know that lust was like light, that it never vanished and could never end – or that it could even be inherited and could be passed on to that angel-faced boy. She deposited five years of delirious passion into his tiny body where it would grow, serene and untamed, and would soon break out.

༈

Umm Salman al-Khattar died peacefully, leaving a nearly twenty-five year old Buthayna all alone in the big house. She'd grown up suddenly and the people who knew her could see how she'd matured. Her almond eyes grew seductive; her wheaten complexion had given way to a bright and faintly ruddy whiteness; her body stretched and filled out. She was engaged to marry her cousin Hussein who'd immigrated to Venezuela. After the October War when the soldier-sons of Sarmada returned from the front, escorting one martyr and five casualties including Hussein – minus the captured or vanished Hamoud – Buthayna got engaged to Hussein al-Nimr. He left for Venezuela eighteen months later with the expectation that Buthayna would join him in the very near future.

One day he came and sat beside her as she was peeling and eating prickly pears and asked her to follow him somewhere more private so they could talk more freely, 'Buthayna, have you ever been in love?'

She answered with a virgin's puffed-up bluster, 'You think you're the only man who loves me?' Then, 'So do you love me?'

Hussein laughed so hard she had to shield her ears from his famous guffawing.

'I fell in love with you just right now.'

He'd noticed the dimples appearing and disappearing on her glorious, smooth cheeks, and her slightly sad, but thoroughly bold face. He moved closer to plant a kiss on her cheek, longing to feel those alluring dimples, and she let him, but only for a moment and then she pushed him away, the unmovable coquette: 'Now have some prickly pear and behave yourself.'

She was deeply in love with Hussein and his departure broke her heart. She was infatuated with his smell, his sense of humour, his looks, his irresistible charm, and the spark of lightning in his downcast eyes and the thunder in his laugh. The day he showed her where the bullet had destroyed half of his left hand, she took the initiative, for the first time, and kissed the old scar. She overwhelmed him after having starved his heart with repeated rejection. She smelt his sweet, permeating scent, she tasted his cruel, astonishingly soft lips, and when she slid her hand through the thick forest of his chest, she felt all earthly security wrap around her and she knew that she wanted to be with this man forever and ever.

His absence caused her days to lengthen and time to slow. She did everything she could to hide the void and blunt the edge of waiting. Although she waited for Hussein, after two years' separation, she'd forgotten what he looked like. And yet she had memorised that crazy desperate look in his eyes and tried to embroider his features onto the faces of her pillows. More than anything else though, her most treasured bliss came when she saw the postman Nasser zipping along on his creaky motorcycle from Poppy Bridge to bring the village news of half of their sons who'd left in recent years for Venezuela, Latin America, Libya and the Gulf.

Nasser the postman would park his motorcycle, take out his

famous chair and plant himself down. He'd begin passing out the letters and most of the time ended up reading the letters out to the recipients in exchange for a gift of food, or clothes or whatever the people had to give. He usually came to Sarmada, where half the houses waited in suspense, twice a month. With every letter, Buthayna lit a candle at the tree Mother of Rams and left a few coins, muttering: 'May your blessings grow, Mother of Rams. Keep him and help him in God's name. I'll bring you a big ram just let me get word that I'm going to join him.'

She lived for Hussein's passion-and-longing-scented letters. She watched over his absence by candlelight, and fought back dejection by making blankets and embroidering. And when on lonely nights, she longed for him, she took the pillow embroidered with his sweet face into her arms and drifted off to sleep, remembering his silk-woven laugh, only to see him in her dreams and wake up in a sweat.

She learnt to spin wool and knit winter sweaters with clever designs. She made baskets out of straw. She decorated the boxes in her house with muslin flowers. She embroidered her family's faces onto her white sheets, and she embroidered Hussein's face dozens of times: smiling Hussein, gruff Hussein, pensive Hussein. She fought against erasure and absence with her embroidery needle, but her hate for Farida remained, clear and distinct. She hated her in the very depths of her soul.

Farida, who'd tried in every way imaginable to make gestures of friendship toward the young girl, had given up and let her be, but she always kept her door open in case the angry young woman eventually settled down.

Farida took it all in stride because she understood that Buthayna was simply searching for something, anything at all, to settle her mind like everyone who claims to believe in God's will, but who are fatalists deep down and expect to understand death's tricks with nothing more than their cool reason. They search for an explanation, for the reasons behind its randomness and the mysterious policy by which it selects its victims. They want to understand its sickle, how it's able to cut down souls and conquer life.

It's an important and peculiar controversy, laced with splendour and resentment. Death reaps and life sows. Death is real and life is but a passing moment. In Farida, Buthayna found both the cause and the causer and so drowned out the questions raised by death in the roar of hate for its cause.

At Umm Salman's funeral, Buthayna sat by her mother's head as the other women, relatives and non-relatives, wailed and mourned and eulogised the deceased. And when they took the body to the men's section to pray over it, Buthayna didn't scream or tear out her hair, she simply laid a kiss upon her mother's cheek and calmly said farewell. Farida was the closest to her out of all the guests and she held her tightly like a sister and walked her back to the al-Khattar family's house.

The forty days of mourning passed uneventfully. Every evening without fail, Farida came to condole with Buthayna, to prepare food for those who came to pay their respects, and to help her with the housework. Six months after Umm Salman passed and eight months after she'd last received a letter from Hussein, loneliness shrouded her heart and she was exhausted. Her eyes were bloodshot, her body sapped, and her mind cautioned that the worst was yet to come. Her troubled soul gave up on the solace of embroidering absent-faces and clutching pillows stuffed with emptiness. The faces she'd created with her adroit needle had become sad and gloomy and began to disappear behind elliptical threads in which the images recurred infinitely.

Farida came to her and took her by the hand and led her back to the shed. She brought her an infusion of anise, camomile and thyme to which she'd added a few other herbs and it put Buthayna into a deep slumber for a whole day and a half. When she eventually woke up, she saw Farida in a different light and when she saw Bulkhayr skipping across the floor of the shed, she was suddenly giddy and guilty. At four and a half, Bulkhayr was an unbelievably cheerful boy. Farida had let his hair grow out and it would stay long like that until he went to school as a vow she'd made at the Shrine of Shihan. That was the saint Farida had chosen out of a great many shrines to become the boy's protector and shield him from all harm.

'Beware the evil eye, Farida. Keep an eye on him and may God protect him for you.'

Buthayna was worried that her envious eye would curse him. He was a charmingly rambunctious boy and he had the kind of brilliant laugh that would scratch your heart. Between the delight of playing with Bulkhayr and waiting for the postman to come, the time passed with a caution mixed with a sharp and stinging worry because her left ear was constantly telling her that bad news was waiting for her.

The postman got to the big house in the evening. He was so experienced that all he had to do was to feel a package to know what was inside. In all honesty, he used to open up the letters masterfully, read them and then seal them back up before he delivered them so he would know how much his tip should be, based on what the message contained. He handed her the letter and quickly left, and as she watched him disappear in the distance, she knew that bad news awaited her. When the postman ran off without even waiting for a tip, you could be sure that the news wasn't just bad, it was catastrophic.

She read the letter through once, and she needed all the strength in the world to go over it again. It was only a few lines long and began, 'Dearest Buthayna':

'By the time you get this letter, I'll be in America. The situation here isn't like you think. Everybody who said that Venezuela was a land of dreams was lying. I don't even know what dreams they were talking about. I'm exhausted, Buthayna, I'm completely worn out. After all these years, I still don't have anything to show for it. I'm going to go try my luck in America. I swear by God and the soil of Sarmada, that you won't leave my thoughts – not even for a moment – but I don't want you to wait for me hopelessly. You're free, Buthayna. Free from the moment this letter reaches you. I hope you find a good man that deserves you and that you forgive me. Please forgive me, Buthayna.'

She read the letter over and over again. Two burning teardrops welled up and slid down her flushed cheeks and she calmly wiped them away, hiding them with the rest of the letter, and from that day forward, her nights stretched mercilessly on without end. She took refuge in her mutilated solitude, rent by the mania of longing, desire and frustration. She spread his letters out around her, stripped off all her clothes, and put his shirt on over her bare skin. She summoned the photos in her mind rubbed bare by her imagination's thumbing and placed a soft pillow between her thighs and sat there, bucking against it. She ran her hands over her body and let out a moan that broke through the stifling stoppage of loneliness and longing. She woke up the next morning and began to collect all the things that had anything to do with him: his letters, his gifts, the sweet photos he'd sent her, and then she lit a fire in the oven and threw in some husks. She made some dough and kneaded it and then she fed the fire with the souvenirs and sat there making loaves of bread from the memories, which only days ago had stubbornly refused to budge.

When she was finished burning everything connected to him, she was left with a stack of pitas, delicious flatbread, and manaqeesh with zaatar, kishk and thick yoghurt. After she was finally done cooking him, or burning him, she took a few bites of those years of renunciation and shared the rest with the neighbours. She wasn't surprised to hear some of them say, 'Thank you so much, Buthayna. Your bread's the most delicious of all.' One of her neighbours told her it felt as if a mysterious burden had been lifted off her chest.

She tried to remember his face, but she couldn't. She was slightly disconcerted to find that her memory held no duplicate. 'How could I have forgotten his scent? He's vanished as if he was never there to begin with.' She discovered that the way to heal the devastation of distance was to gather everything, chew it up and give it all away. She exiled him from her heart, although in truth, she'd only disguised him. For a moment, she felt she'd been emptied of everything that had to do with him, blank just as she ought to be, renewed and awaiting the blooming days, which signalled to her that they were coming, now that the traces of that bitter separation had all been wiped away and the colourful trunk of her fennel tree-beloved had been burnt up in the oven's fire.

Her body was vigorous once more and the pores that had stifled her and drowned her body in an ocean of longing reopened. She wrapped herself in yearning's silk and took comfort in the vague hope that one day in the warm Caribbean sun, her body would uncover itself for her departed lover and thaw, shedding off the torpor of frozen passion. But he was squirreled away inside of her, deeply rooted and every time she destroyed him, he was born again. She was forced to ask herself a painful question: what did she want from him: a story or a child? If it was a love story she wanted, then, by all means, give it balance, give it colour. Let the picture be distorted, let the joy sit uneasy, that, after all, is the circumstance of a woman in love, that's the inevitable result of his great absence and there was no reason why she couldn't shift her affection toward someone else. But if it was a child she wanted, then why not simply get pregnant by someone else? Why not simply marry whatever man would give her a child?

She arrived at a peculiar conclusion: a child is an ending, and every story begins with a potential child. She found her own wisdom compelling, and it seemed to relieve her of her anxious burden. She'd never once dreamt of being a mere womb for his child, but rather the heroine of his romance, and that realisation took the faintest edge off the pain. She packed up some of her things and went over to Farida's shed. She didn't say a word about it; they just exchanged some frantic village gossip as Farida lit the stove and made a pot of yerba mate, and then they sat there, drinking green cupful after green cupful of yerba mate flavoured with lemon and cardamom.

With her veteran woman's eye, Farida could see how Buthayna had matured even as she tried to evade her glance, chipping in eagerly and washing down the floor of the shed as she sang, or to put it more precisely, keened funereally. Farida prepared her a herbal mixture to cure heartache and threw in a few special ingredients that she kept around for special moments like that one. She wished she still had some grief-milk left. After the mixture had steeped for two and a half hours, she strained it and added a pinch of wormwood to heal the spasms of loss. She brought her concoction over on a wicker tray and poured it into a ceramic cup. She gave Buthayna a motherly, or big-sisterly, look.

'I'm not feeling well, Farida,' said Buthayna. 'I don't feel at all well.'

'I know, my dear. I know. You'll feel better very soon.'

She fed her a sandwich of thick yoghurt and mint leaves with her own hands and then told her to drink the drink down in one go. Although Farida had got rid of all her grief-milk, she still knew which herbs could cure a broken heart. In only a few minutes, Buthayna's tears began pouring freely. She let out all the anticipation, everything it had brought with it and everything surrounding it. She flushed it out of her heart's womb with those tears she'd locked away ever since the sobbing plague had struck Sarmada.

She cried until her eyes were parched. Her soul was bathed and stretched wide open to force out all those pillow-embroidered faces and to announce a new beginning. She ran home and rummaged through the granary. She pulled out the box that contained al-Hazred's book on the secrets of the dead and then she told Farida all the secrets that were hidden in the depths of her soul and how she'd almost killed everyone in Sarmada with the soothsayer of Kanakir's arsenic. Farida took the box of manuscripts and hid it in the chaff store to look through later, now though she turned all her attention to Buthayna, who took great comfort in her presence. Those were days of confession, sobbing and purification for them both.

At the end of the week, the two women sat together in the evening after Bulkhayr had settled into bed and decided to have a sugaring party to get rid of their unwanted hair, as a parallel means of washing themselves clean of love's burnt-up gunk and purifying it in the depilatory pain. Farida had suggested the idea in order to get Buthayna out of her bereavement once and for all, and also to make sure that the slate was wiped clean because she knew instinctively that two women could never make up and clear the air of the womanly hatred between them unless and until they were naked together.

Farida heated up three potfuls of water to which she added lemon peel, quinine leaves and mint as the bathroom filled with steam. Buthayna was making up sticky strips of beeswax, rose water and lemon juice. 'Do you have any ginger?' she called to Farida.

'Look up on the shelf.' Buthayna radiated joy as she ran her eyes over the stopped up, long-necked bottles of spices arranged on the shelves, so she didn't even notice the suspicious looks she was getting as she ran her hands over the curves of her body.

Farida was watching Buthayna stealthily from the corner of the bathroom. She looked exhausted from making the depilatory recipe, dressed in her yellow blouse, and you could clearly make out her vigorously rising and falling breasts and protruding nipples under her blouse. She felt a sudden frisson in her blood and when Buthayna turned around, her eyes fixed on her full and supple bottom as it swayed. 'Lord help me,' she muttered pleadingly. 'What's wrong with you, Farida?' she snapped at herself, rebuking her mind for the surprise of her body's summons. Desire is blind and its true motives unknowable. She did a quick accounting and found she'd never – not once – longed for another woman before. So how come she'd suddenly fallen into this notion's grasp? How had it infiltrated a soul made pure by repentance and motherhood? She cursed herself, cursed the curse of the body until she finally let out something very near the audible, warning herself: 'Don't, Farida. Don't you dare. Don't even think about it.' She sat down and began to recite some supplications and verses that were supposed to drive away a husbandless woman's demons, although only she and her worried soul could hear her.

Buthayna broke in on her whispered prayers: 'You'll help me, won't you?' she asked, undressing, getting ready to depilate her pubic area. Farida needed every last atom in her brain to turn down the temptation-soaked invitation and tear her gaze from Buthayna's vulva.

'No, I've got to cook something for Bulkhayr. I'll help you next time.' She didn't want to risk going any nearer the danger she'd sworn she'd keep away from, so she left Buthayna to get ready and to remove her unwanted hair and to spend the better part of the evening in the bathroom, where – kept company by her invigorating pain – she began to sing.

Farida snuggled her son and tried with every fibre of her being to expel the voice in her head that evening. She would awash in erotic dreams of Buthayna, which caused her to wake up, panicked and damp. Her mood showed no sign of improving so she finally made up her mind. She told Buthayna: 'You've got to go back to your place. It isn't good to leave the house empty.'

Having won her temporary reprieve from loss, Buthayna seethed with life. Despite being kicked out, or Farida's surprising, and slightly cruel, request from out of nowhere, she tried not to make a big deal out of it and as she was making her way back to the al-Khattar family home, she said to herself, 'Farida's got a point. It isn't right to neglect the family home like this.'

Hyperactive Bulkhayr planted smiles wherever he went, but over time Sarmada's adulation evolved into cloying boredom. No one ever scolded him and every single thing he did earned him praise and affection. It was constant: anyone who saw him would either kiss him, or joke with him, or give him a treat, or buy him one, and anyone who'd been away would have to return with a gift for Bulkhayr. News about him was greedily sought after with the excuse that his father had been a war hero and a martyr, and a good teacher to boot, and that he had done the right thing by all.

In all truth though, he never felt the slightest bit exceptional in life, except that he had two penises and didn't know which one he ought to pee out of. Bulkhayr cheerfully entered the first grade shortly before his sixth birthday, dressed in the khaki uniform with the Baath-scout neckerchief and his leather satchel, which had once belonged to Hamoud the geography teacher, in hand. Farida, who was letting him go out for the first time unsupervised, found the house suddenly desolate, and she felt that her new life, the one she'd embraced and got used to and which had blunted her claws with the file of monotony, had begun to sharpen her feelings, to hone their ability to scar, but she kept on with her new life all the same.

Her extraordinary talent for optimism, for taking part in celebrations, and for conscientiously and generously giving her time and energy amazed everyone. She watched as the fruit of her womb grew up before her eyes and was filled with cheeky pride as well as great misgiving for when she peered into time's gaze, she could see how far it stretched and how unpredictable it was – its every moment both a beginning and an end. She could see that time was divided into two paths: one brought things and the other carried them away. Her own life was short and it was headed down a single path now that she'd closed off all the portals to the past and blocked them up with the tree of her passion, which she'd cut down and chopped up to fuel the fire of time. Yet as soon as she'd embraced an asceticism of the body, ridiculing it for its triviality, new inanities cropped up: how could she give him – this child embodiment of the past – the features of the present? Down which paths should she lead him? Up toward God and unity and the void or down into the secret underground where he'd learn how to confront what was found on the surface? She decided she'd wait until the time came and would deal with whatever was going to happen as it happened. She locked up the flocks of suspicion and all it spawned in her ribcage and lo the flapping ceased.

She was the first single mother in the area and a lot of people knew it. They cheered her for not having killed her foetus and managing to secure a cover story to allow him to forge a life in a place ill with fanaticism and shame. He once asked her out of the blue, 'How come everyone else has a dad and I don't?'

'Oh, you're father was a hero, my love, and he was martyred in the war.' She pointed to Hamoud's photograph on the wall, which had a shiny black ribbon round one corner of the frame. That answer didn't really satisfy him and he slowly began to realise that there was something different about him in addition to the thing between his legs.

Buthayna calmly tried to dismiss anyone who tried to get close to her because she couldn't stand the sight of any of Sarmada's men now that Hussein had forsaken her. Just the thought of her foolish Penelope-vigil was humiliating. She knew full well that he was never coming back and that she'd be condemned to wait her entire life, no matter how hard she struggled to escape its clinging, and she came to realise that the trenches, which desire ploughed through her body, would no longer be fulfilled by self-pleasuring alone. But at the same time, she felt that her body would be wasted on the boorish men around her, so she embraced the idea of spinsterhood with an open mind.

One day when she saw Bulkhayr playing near the valley, she called to him and he ran over. She sent him to the shop to buy a few things and he was an expert at running errands by now: getting a few coins in return, showing off how wonderfully fast he could run, wowing the adults with his record times. When he returned, flushed and panting, she asked him about school and caught sight of something angelic bubbling up to the surface of his face, rustling awake her own sleeping demons. She didn't want the conversation to end. 'What did you learn today?'

'We got to the letter *ghayn*', he answered earnestly. غ

'So you know how to write the letter *ghayn* now?' she asked.

'I know half the letters,' he answered with boyish pride. 'I can write your name if you want.'

She smiled gaily and kissed him on the cheek near to his mouth and as she grazed his soft lips, she shuddered inexplicably, her body joining stealthily in. She grabbed a notepad and pencil and sat him down on the ground. 'Show me how you write my name. If you write it right, I'll give you a sweet.' He began showing off his school skills and wrote her name out phonetically: *Buthayn* (بثين). After a moment's thought, he made it: *Buthaynat* (بثينت). She laughed and changed the final letter to a silent T (بثينة).

'I wrote the letter N (ن) even though we didn't   learn it yet.'

Was it his innocence that drew her to him or was it simply the emptiness that had stretched cobwebs across the corners of her life? She watched his angelic face as he concentrated intently on the notepad, his fingers smudged with lead, and grieved for her brother who'd been struck down in the prime of life. What if this boy had been his son, would she have loved him even more? Or perhaps less? Where did an awareness of bloodlines or bonds, whether sacred or profane, even come from?

She arrested her troubled thoughts, faked a weak smile, and mumbled, 'The N is very good. Let me teach you how to write the rest of the alphabet.' She took his little hand and drew a semi-circle, adding a dot up at the top (ن). Then she wrote out a few words on his notepad: N (نون), fire (نار), women (نساء), light (نور), and told him to copy them.

After an hour of tireless housework, she was finally done. As she was drying her hands, she was struck by a vague demonic anxiety so she poured some grape molasses into a white bowl and licked her finger after wiping the rim of the jar. The sweet stung, or rather stirred, something inside her. She went back in and saw him, focused – as happy as could be – on copying the words one after the other.

'Finished!' he shouted. 'I wrote all the words.'

As a little diversion, he both amused and saddened her with his overflowing innocence and beauty. 'You deserve something sweet,' she said, dipping her finger into the bowl. 'Here, open your mouth.'

She placed her finger in his mouth and he closed his lips around it. He began sucking on her finger, his eyes shut, the words being branded in his memory with the taste on his tongue, and it tickled her right index finger and caused blood to rush into her breast. She removed her finger, gave him a quarter lira, and sent him on his way, driving out the ludicrous imaginings that had filled her head.

Two days later, he took his schoolbooks and homework and went to see her. She was taken aback by the sight of this rosy-faced boy, carrying a schoolbag bigger than he was and a worksheet blazoned with a jotted note in red: *Well done and keep it up.* He spoke to her confidently, but with earnest pleading: 'I want you to teach me the rest of the alphabet, Auntie.' She found the combination of his angel face and intent affecting, so she sat him down on the ground and made him take out his pens and paper.

'At school, you get a "Good Work!", but here I'm going to give you a lick for every letter you write correctly.' And then she laughed but it trailed off into abrupt doubts:

What are you doing? Were you actually waiting for him? And if he hadn't come, would you have felt some great void that only this little rabbit could fill? Be honest, Buthayna, is it really true that the only thing that can change the uninterrupted desert of your life is a visit from him? Could you really bring yourself to taint his innocence? What's this gaping emptiness you're feeling, Buthayna? What is it?

Her own laughter took her unawares, and in its prolonged abundance, all questions and desires were curtailed.

He was busy carefully making his handwriting as nice as he could as he copied out the list of words she wrote on his sheet of paper, bringing his face closer to hers to smell her redolent, fragrant scent, and innocently watch her protruding, quivering breasts.

After he'd finished his assignment, she brought out the dish of grape molasses and dipped her finger in it. She brought her finger up to his mouth, but when he tried to nibble at it, she gently pulled away. He followed her finger as if hypnotised, while she unbound her breasts with her left hand and brought them out into the open. She brought her finger to her breast and splashed it with grape molasses as he, like a little puppy, followed the sugary trail and the bosom taste he'd been weaned from more than three and a half years earlier. He stuck out his tongue, licking roundly flawless a letter M (م) unlike any other. Once the wine-coloured blouse had been removed, she could paint her perky nipple and say, 'Have some molasses' in her best Arabic, mocking the tone of the teacher she was supposed to be.

He came nearer the rosy nipple, doused in a liquid that obscured the glowing white, and he ran his lips over it and took it into his mouth, and then out. He could hear the uncertainty in her voice, the way it quavered. She dipped her finger into the dish and rubbed it over the other nipple. He grabbed onto them and begun to suck, moving back and forth between them. With an uncanny and unending patience, he crawled above her as she lay back against two pillows.

She began dipping two fingers and drawing circles from her breasts down to her stomach. He followed the sour scent of grape molasses, like a giddy wolf pup, licking unremittingly. She drew the alphabet across her stomach, first the letter A (ا), and he repeated, 'The letter A' as he licked.

With his tongue, he licked up the alphabet of her body. 'The letter B (ب): one dot under. The letter T (ت): two dots above.'

She repeated the letters he'd learnt that day by heart and tongue;

the letters tasted of grape molasses in his mouth. The sticky liquid settled in her navel and overflowing ventured downward. She slipped her khaki-coloured skirt off and broke all the bonds of equivocation as she removed her panties – white with tiny blue hearts. The molasses spilt down over her loins and he went searching for the sweetness in the sprouting hair. It smelt like the wheat harvest and cooked molasses. He slithered down between her thighs and instinct alone led him to the syrupy volcano that awaited him. He started by tasting her labia dyed dark by the grape molasses. She grabbed the back of his head and then he stuck his tongue out and plunged it inside her to take his virgin taste as his nose rested against her pubic arch. She tugged his hair and pressed him down between her thighs, pulling him in deeply. He devoured the moisture between her thighs, submerged down to the very dregs.

He wanted to penetrate her with his face, and with his teeth, and his tongue, and his nose that was buried in the trembling damp. She pulled him up and down and up again until his entire face ran with the sticky liquid flowing plentifully from between her thighs. He stopped suddenly and it was as if he were simply about to burst with laughter. He heard her fiery moans and asked, 'Is everything all right, Auntie?' She seized the back of his neck and pulled his head back down between her thighs, grinding against his face, not giving a damn about the laughter, which had turned to fear and unmistakable tears as his angel face was transformed into that of a pale, molasses-smeared lizard.

His first year of school went by and the grape molasses lessons continued even though her irresistible instinct to possess the child gnawed at her and her dream of becoming a mother constantly lashed at her soul. She wanted a child more than she wanted a husband. It was a perverse desire that jarred the walls of her empty womb, demanding she fill it, and yet, at the same time, some enigmatic emotion led her to continue with the molasses lessons. She thought it over for a long while until in a single instant, her true feelings and motives became fleetingly clear. Was she really just trying to get revenge on Farida by corrupting her child?

She couldn't come up with a clear answer, but she resolved to stop regardless because her feelings of deadbeat guilt drowned the pleasure of it in sin. She screamed at him, escorted him out, and slammed the door shut behind her with a determination she wanted her desire to take note of. He stood there on the doorstep, carrying his schoolbag, and pounded and pounded, bawling and panting and shouting: 'Open up, Auntie! Open up! Please, Auntie, open up!' She put her fingers in her ears and refused to give in to the insistent wish to open the door and hold him and wipe away his tears and shower him with all the affection she could muster. It was pure torture until he eventually left. She watched his short, slouching form walk past. He would stop to look back and then carry on as the big schoolbag weighed him down so that he could barely manage it. She gasped when he stumbled on some rocks, but he got back up, dusted off his clothes, wiped his teary eyes, and continued on. That last sight of him etched itself on her mind and she clung to it for the next decade.

That evening she went to see Joumana al-Rayyash and told her that she'd agree to marry her brother, Saloum. She returned home and took a shower so hot it nearly scalded her skin. She didn't cry.

Before the wedding, Buthayna sat with Saloum al-Rayyash and looked with her scorn-tinged heart into his eyes, which oozed fretfulness every time he blinked. She examined his long, soft and unsettling fingers and embraced him silently, which ended up confusing him more than it should have. His questions and conversation-openers all failed to drive away the mocking smile that made him so uneasy and so vulnerable to jest. But when he started telling her his stories, he was able to hide her ridicule and make it into something more like listening. He wanted to put her fears to rest, or more likely his own, by telling her the stories of his noteworthy family. He wanted to be as candid as possible, in a way befitting a former communist, a high-calibre mathematics graduate, and an intellectual who supported the materialist theory of the world and historical determinism. Though when he spoke there was no hiding the petty bourgeois inside him, or to put it more plainly: he had all the traits of a liberal feudal lord and it made him the constant target of his comrades' criticisms, but he still managed to lure the broken-hearted Buthayna into listening. He didn't care what anyone else thought. All he wanted was to break down the barriers separating him from this sexy, strong and fierce girl who plagued his heart with hope's panic.

After he got the chance to go to the Gulf, he couldn't give a damn about the accusations they tried to smirch him with: small-minded opportunist, free-rider, callow lefty. He walked out on the circles of communists and the enlightened after he made a point of order at a meeting, interrupting a raving comrade who was saying that: 'The Muslim Brotherhood and the government are both evil and we have to give priority to putting an end to the most dangerous of the two. As it stands right now, the most dangerous evil is the Brotherhood because what they want is to turn Syria into an Islamic state, and they're going to wipe out all the esoteric sects because that's what their draconian authorities, such as Ibn Taymiyya and Ibn al-Jawzi, have always told them to do over a long history of suppressing esoteric sects who'd made great progress compared to the underdevelopment of classical Islam.'

It was sectarian scare-mongering dressed up in a Marxist critique and Saloum couldn't take the bullshit any longer. He placed his right fist against his left palm and rose to make a point of order. He demanded he be allowed to speak: 'Comrade Lenin used to say that his fight wasn't with capitalism, it was with the lice infesting the heads of Russian children. I don't think our fight ought to be with the ruling class, or with the government, or even with America and the Arab reactionaries, and not even with Israel above all else because everything we're fighting is connected and it'll all collapse once we liberate ourselves from within. Our fight ought to be with ourselves. Before we set up our coat rack and start hanging up defeats and excuses and evaluations about who's more dangerous than who and theories about the future, we've got to start with ourselves as individuals, as a party, or as cells in a progressive movement, and ask ourselves, "Where are we right now?"

'We skip over illiteracy and poverty. We ignore individuals, and the rights of people and their dignity, and even life itself as a legal principle. Instead we agitate and call for resistance and sacrifice. Our fallen are "martyrs" just like in the religious code we're trying to uproot or tear down. Comrade, the retreat to religion is flourishing because there's no such thing as justice, and because individuals' sense of self and self-worth is equal to zero. When the earth is undifferentiated misery, heaven will thrive. When ideas are impotent and strange and naïve and they have nothing to do with reality, well, then all people have left is magic, and heaven and houris. Or else they can only volunteer to become fuel for leaders' fires.

'Me, personally, I don't want to be anyone's sacrifice, not just so I can substitute someone new to oppress me and deprive me of my right to life and self-expression; my right not to be part of a group, but a private individual whose personal freedom is holiest of all; my right to break out of the sectarian flock, out of the party flock – it's just a different sect with a different vocabulary – out of the flock of the independent nation ruled by a colonialist whose eyes are only slightly less blue, out of the flock of God and those who use him and make up laws to control me and keep me from reaching out to Him if I want to.

'Comrade, if we should toil for the sake of the nation and good and freedom, then we should toil for love and freedom, for our rights and dignity. And beyond that, religious fundamentalism and dictatorship are two sides of the same coin. As soon as the Arab regimes fall, the fundamentalist lie will collapse, too. But it's not you all or the other Arab political parties that are going to

bring down the regimes. No, you're all made up of the same ingredients. The regimes will fall because of something no one will see
coming: when people stop using the imported language of others
and discover their own. And when they do, they're going to leave
the whole lot of you behind. You won't believe your eyes. You're
the ones who want a revolution, but it's the people who are going
to invent new ways of change once they find their own language
again. The language you stole from them because you've never
known how to talk to regular folks.'

Despite the uproar from his comrades and their attempts to
interrupt him, he carried on pouring out everything that had
pooled in his heart over all those years of pathetic, wasted pain
and rage. He shouted at them, 'Your hate for the dictator runs so
deep, it's blinded you and now you're beginning to resemble him.
Dictatorship has corrupted us all and more importantly than that,
it's driven a wedge between us and our people; it's separated us
from ourselves. Not to worry though, another generation will give
birth to revolution. It definitely won't be us. We're just a bunch of
hollow hacks, We're full of self loathing more than anything else.'
He left before they could kick him out.

He began writing love poems to Buthayna, although she'd
already turned him down a number of times. Comparing him
cursorily to her manly Hussein, she found him a university kid,
who had a different way of talking about Sarmada and she could
never tell whether he was happy or sad. He was outwardly fake
with people and he was torn between his cultural elitism and his
true nature, which she soon uncovered as he went on talking. He
shared some snippets from the history of his family, who were
famous throughout the mountain region, pairing truth with the
incredible, but ultimately it was one of those Sarmadan tales that
provided the village with its uncanny talent for telling its own
story and gave anyone who encountered it the freedom to tell it as
he or she pleased. The truth was that Saloum's story had managed
to grip conceited Buthayna's attention so she turned to look up

at Windhill, her eyes full of the sarcasm she marshalled so well, tinted by a mysterious glimmer. Behind the hill, lay the Mountain of the Bearded Shaykh; it got its name from the abiding snow that resembled an old man's bright white beard and shined back at her. She turned to look at him, imploring him to tell the story and everything else he'd been unable to say before. As Saloum's sadness-troubled voice spilled out on the roof of the al-Khattar family home, the dish of grape molasses went untouched and the cup of yerba mate was sipped at only once because his hands were busy wandering through the air as he began to remember.

The story goes that al-Bunni, Saloum al-Rayyash's great-great-great-grandfather, was mad about hunting and he set off one snowy morning, concealing a wounded leg that had begun to suppurate. He took his rifle, saddled up his horse, packed provisions for seven days, and headed westward toward the rugged ground. Al-Bunni, whose infamy reached all the way to Istanbul, had cost the Ottoman garrison more than fifty Janissaries and years of wounded pride, until they finally decided to appoint him the unofficial chief of the area from the northern edge of the rocky wasteland all the way to Hebariyeh. Sarmada became a symbol of anti-Ottoman rebellion: Sarmadans paid no taxes and their sons never served in the Janissary Corps. He opened up his home to the hungry from across the Levant during the famine and its rooms became shelters for refugees, help-seekers and those who were wanted at the Ottoman gallows from all over the Arabian Peninsula and the Levant. He was big and tall and had the kind of handlebar moustache a falcon could perch on. He was a hyena hunter, a friend to wolves and a tracker, and he knew the deserts of the Lajat and its trails. He had memorised the secrets of the great rocks and their hiding places. Settling down in one place was something he just couldn't stomach so no sooner had he turned up somewhere, that he'd be heading off again, and he only ever stayed put when someone came to him to plead for protection or when a guest had nowhere else to turn and was forced to take refuge with that taciturn, irascible, crack-shot rebel. He had kohled eyes and plaited hair hanging down over his back and shoulders. He never shirked a raid, or threat, or point of honour no matter where it might lead him. He was accompanied by a troop of roving kohl-eyed, plait-haired riders who were greeted with prayers and ululations in all the deserts and villages of the mountains they visited. They symbolised the bold streak of independence that ran through the Lajat.

Al-Bunni wasn't looking to get his hands on power or a covenant by rebelling against every last outside power that tried to interrupt the harmony of the place. He already knew he was the last male in his line. Nevertheless, he wanted to solve the riddle, or at least to break it down so he could understand why and maybe even manage to decipher the code before his nebulous destiny was fulfilled. That same destiny that had nursed him as a baby – his family's highest priority; a priority that couldn't even be discussed until he was weaned at the age of five, having sucked the breasts of six wet-nurses dry.

'He went in the direction of the Fatin Springs deep in the wasteland of the Lajat,' said the shepherd, answering al-Bunni's wife, Mitha, whose heart had been heavy for days. She was, of course, perfectly used to his habit of coming and going and she understood that nowhere on earth felt more like home to him than the back of his pure-bred horse, Kaheela, which carried him over the wasteland's rocky carpet and through the boulder-wilderness to the distant borders of his longing. Thus she steeled herself for many teary years and she wept for al-Bunni until the coal-black of her irises leached to a bluish-green. The shepherd recalled, 'We were together, me and al-Bunni, and he shot at a falcon. He did exactly what his grandfather did years ago, but the only way to catch a falcon is to trick it and if it does end up getting caught, it'll raise its head high and plunge its sharp beak straight through its heart. It refuses to grow decrepit, so when it starts getting old, it circles up and up in the air toward the sun and then comes barrelling down in a suicidal free-fall.' The shepherd was showing off his knowledge and his conversation drifted off course, wading through details that meant nothing to a pregnant woman whose husband had disappeared in the enchanted rocky wasteland.

As Mitha listened to the shepherd's story, her eyes filled with tears, but she stopped her sobbing momentarily when she heard him say that he'd heard al-Bunni talking to the falcon and that he'd washed out its wounded wing and cared for it over those three days, and then poured gunpowder on the wound and cauterised it with a glowing knife-blade, and then he let it go. It flew away after circling around al-Bunni's head several times. It dropped him a feather it had plucked out of its breast, and he grabbed the feather and waited and then another feather fell, and a third, and then a fourth. 'I heard him say, "Fate's given us another chance. We're going to have sons"', said the shepherd.

'What else did he say? Do you remember? How did he look? Where did he go?'

'That's all, I swear. He told me to go back and he stayed in the wasteland.' Mitha suddenly remembered her old fears of al-Bunni being the last in the al-Rayyash line. The exact same thing had happened to his grandfather, except that he'd killed a sacred falcon during the glut and the birds prayed that his line would be wiped out. Al-Bunni was the last of his line according to those who knew the secrets. 'It has to be a sign from God,' she said to herself. She crossed through a bemusing wasteland, over obscure deserts, in thrall to a heart accustomed to loss. She took a pinch of salt and made for the spring. The same spring that Azza Tawfiq had known about. The spring that was the last thing Hela Mansour ever remembered. She threw the silver grains in, repeating her wish: first that she would have a son and then that the one who'd disappeared would return, but only if that were possible, because she had a hunch that the power of the spring was only ever enough for one wish.

Al-Bunni disappeared, or to be more precise, he followed the example of his forefathers: when they felt death drawing near, they set out for the faraway deserts and died there, graveless, offering their bodies up to the scavenging animals. The old wound in his thigh had been torn open once more and gangrene was consuming his body. He didn't want anyone's pity; he couldn't stand to die surrounded by other people's humiliating compassion. He didn't want anyone to see him in pain or wasting away. He'd lived as a free man, outside the jurisdiction of natural laws, and he wanted to die just as he'd lived.

Mitha, who was pregnant, gave birth to Shrouf, who begat Qoftan, who begat Shaheen and Shaheen married a woman who was called Saliha al-Kanj. She gave him four daughters: Fatima, Sara, Maryam and Rahma, and he continued to wait for a son, but it was in vain. Five sons were snatched away by death before their third birthdays for reasons that maybe the holy birds knew, or maybe the soothsayer of Kanakir could guess, so Saliha al-Kanj turned to the woman who possessed the power of the birds for help.

'Please. You have to help me, I want a son who will live.'

'It's all in God's hands. You'll have a son only if it's your destiny.'

'I've tried every remedy and offering. I've gone to every imam and soothsayer, but there's no use: we haven't had a boy despite all our trying. We don't want the family line to be cut off.'

She examined her fresh face and blue eyes, and began to think. After a period of silence that to Saliha al-Kanj seemed to last a lifetime, she spoke: 'A son will come. Give him a name with the word God in it, have him baptised in the Christians' font, and take him to the shrines of six Druze saints, so that he shall survive.' Then in a rasping voice, with manufactured piety, she added, 'God willing … Go on, now, madam.' She called to Saliha al-Kanj as she rose to leave, 'O believer …'

'Is everything alright?'

'When the boy comes, don't let him out of your sight for a moment. A moment's distraction and it'll all be over: forget about

BUTHAYNA

day and night, forget about the bathroom and the call of nature.
Don't take your eyes off him, not for a moment. He must be protected from death by wakefulness, there can't be any dozing off
or distraction, and he must remain purer than pure. He shall be
watched and pure and clean, free of the slightest indecency, free of
even a single sin. And then as soon as he reaches puberty, find him
a wife. You mustn't forget. Now, go.'

Saliha al-Kanj gathered herself up and left. A secret bliss
moved within her and with her every exhalation, worry flowed
out on the breath of fear. Izz Allah arrived to a chorus of prayers
and was carried from Sarmada's baptismal waters to the Druze
shrines. Saliha raised him God-fearingly: matching every inch
he grew with an offering, starting with the Mother of Rams tree
and then taking him to the shrines of Ammar ibn Yasser and
the venerable Abed Mar and Shaykh al-Balkhi, the great Sufi,
and then to Ayn al-Zaman and the grave of Abel and the tomb
of John the Baptist in the Umayyad Mosque and the Mosque of
the great Shaykh Muhi al-Din ibn Arabi. Every six months she
offered a sacrifice and divided it up among the shrines, which
she visited barefoot and bare-hearted, imploring God's saints to
protect her only son.

The boy remained under constant surveillance the whole time,
showered with implacable love to the point of mania. It turned
into a pitched battle between a desire for life and the power of
death, which Saliha had fought all alone in the beginning. When
sleep began to weigh on her eyelids, she'd assign her two daughters
to watch the boy only to wake up in terror after a brief nap. He
grew up happily, and her insomnia grew, too, along with him until
people started calling her the 'Two-lifer' because she never slept,
neither at night nor in the daytime. Saliha al-Kanj had accepted
the wisdom of what the soothsayer of Kanakir had told her: death
comes when your back is turned. It slips through negligence.
People don't die when they're being watched. Death only comes
when everyone is distracted. Her neighbour Umm Saeed told her

about her husband, and confirmed the fortune teller's wisdom: 'He asked for some water so I walked over to the water jug and came back, but the depositor had already collected his deposit! Dear me! I turned my back for just a moment and he was gone. He died thirsty. God keep you, Abu Saeed.'

'I swear by the five cosmic principles, the soul departs in silence.'

Zolaykha al-Joudi stepped in to cut off the mindless conversation: 'Is that the same Abu Saeed who we mourned with the dirge that went:

An old man has died,
And the village mourns a life,
We've lost poor Abu Saeed
who fucked donkeys before he had a wife.

These never-ending conversations helped Saliha al-Kanj fight back the ghoul of time until the family heir was all grown up and the curse of the sacred bird had been broken. The people of Sarmada continued to visit the al-Rayyash family and pass the time, and they even organised supervision shifts to help Saliha protect her child from unforeseen death.

The plan succeeded and Izz Allah was rescued from the claws of prophecy. His younger sister, Rahma, was taken out of school before she'd even finished second grade so she could make sure that her precious brother went on living, shielded by secret amulets, the name of God, and bloodshot, death-defying eyes. As soon as Izz Allah had entered upon his sixteenth spring, he began to consider his marriage to Futoun al-Hamad. She was fifteen, just returning from high school, carrying her leather schoolbag decorated with colourful buttons and embroidery. She had her braided black hair up in a ponytail and if you'd stretched it out, it would've just about reached her knees. Her face was white, tinged with red and innocence. She had a sharp, impudent tongue that would cut anyone who dared go near her pride. The thing Futoun found

140

most hurtful of all, though, was not being the first at something. She used to lead a gang of boys and girls and would challenge them to different contests: jumping, jumping with your feet tied together, swimming, and so on. She was the first girl to wear a short, knee-length skirt and a tank-top in Sarmada and everyone made excuses for that girl. She got away with things that no one else could get away with.

'What? You think you're Futoun, Jabir's daughter, now?' That was the question the adults asked when one of the girls did something that broke with convention or wore something that exposed part of their legs.

It was because she was known to be a spitfire and also because she was the eldest grandchild of Abu Jabir Hazim al-Hamad, one of the great revolutionaries and someone who understood the Nakba through and through because he'd fought alongside Izz al-Din al-Qassam and then during the General Strike in 1936 and he'd been promoted to lieutenant in the Arab Liberation Army. He was held as a political prisoner throughout the period of unification with Egypt because he quickly realised that Pan-Arabism was just a naïve dream that meant nothing in the real world and that what unified the Arabs couldn't be legislated into a distorted union. Hazim al-Hamad showered his granddaughter with affection, or to quote: she was the only person who could touch his wounds and she proceeded to set down – on eleven cassette tapes – the memoirs of this man, who died aged nine years older than the century. He told her the secrets of the Nakba and cautioned her that the Syrian people could never unite with others, no matter how noble the intentions.

Returning from school, her feet were wet because she'd cut across the swirling valley with Ismaeel's son, Na'el, the boldest boy in the village. She was in a foul mood because she'd been unable to jump more than three rocks – and he'd seen this with his own eyes. When she couldn't stand his teasing anymore, she grabbed him by the jacket, jostled him, and dared him to go on mocking her. When he tried to defend himself, she slapped him, and when he returned the slap, she grabbed a rock and hit him. His clothes were covered in blood. Then she cursed at his sister, who tried to rescue him from her lunatic claws.

When she returned home, she tried to hide her white face made red by the slap, and her hands, which were soiled with mud and Na'el's blood, but her eyes were busy trying to figure out what was going on. Her house was full of strangers and Khayzuran, one of Izz Allah's female relatives, welcomed her with ululation, congratulations and blessings. Years later, she told her son about that day, which she'd never been able to forget.

'Little by little, I began to understand what was happening: they'd decided to marry me off. The weird thing was that I didn't object or throw a fit. Of course, they'd already put together a bribe to shut me up: a trip to Damascus to eat ice cream at Bekdash as well as some new clothes, including two skirts that fell above the knee with hems made out of transparent muslin made to look like flowers and three tank tops, along with two tins of Haurani semolina cakes.

'But it wasn't the bribe that got me to go along with it all, or the fact that my grandfather Hamza had agreed to it, or my father's silent congratulations. It was just a strange desire to have a gold ring on my finger before all the other girls in the village. I just had to be first.'

The wedding took place six months later. At first, she thought the marriage was just one big prank and that it would soon be over, but eventually the temptation to discover what the world of the body was about, to get answers to forbidden questions, to know the amazing thrill she'd heard so many of Sarmada's young married women talking about, eased and encouraged her acceptance.

The bride was brought to the wedding on a white horse like a princess, wearing a fez adorned with gold coins and over it a gauzy white headscarf, and a dress of velvet decorated with natural silk. Every last girl in Sarmada was jealous of her. The wedding was attended by all the different mountain communities and was a mix of Islamic, Druze and Christian rituals.

It was only when she arrived at the gate of her new house and Izz Allah helped her down from the horse, that she realised exactly what she'd got herself into. She wasn't on her way to a palace of airy pleasures, but rather to a den of acts antithetical to her innocence. She missed her friends and her games. She wanted to turn back, to put an end to the exhausting hubbub, to run away from all those celebrating guests, to take refuge in the nearest wheat field and outlast whoever came looking for her. But Izz Allah had already walked over to help her down.

She pushed his hand away and said as loudly as she could, 'Move your hand, you piece of shit. I can get down myself!' The sentence froze the young, seventeen year-old groom, who'd been afflicted with this truculent girl, to the spot. He was paralysed with embarrassment and found he couldn't retreat from the guests' eyes.

Then Khayzuran shouted, 'Slap her toothless, the little bitch!'

Futoun gripped the horse's halter tightly in preparation for setting off far away and answered her, 'You! Why don't you eat shit, you whore?'

Those were the last two insults she ever said in public.

Izz Allah failed middle school for the third time because he discovered that the topography of Futoun's body was more deserving of his attention than the geography of the Arab world in his textbook and that her dizzy-making singing was easier to learn than the rules of Arabic poetry.

Saliha al-Kanj imposed a tough regime on the new family. She was anxious for an heir and wanted Futoun to get pregnant straightaway, so she set down a strict diet and subjected her daughter-in-law to monthly examinations. She was constantly asking about her periods and making certain for herself that they were, in fact, doing 'it' on fertile days. At the end of every monthly cycle, she waited with bated breath for the girl to be late, but she was always disappointed.

She forced Izz Allah to eat honey mixed with asafoetida and nuts and she prepared him special dishes that were supposed to boost fertility. She held the headstrong girl to a military schedule of eating, drinking, sleeping, laundry and bathing, until the young couple got totally fed up and decided they'd confront her together. Futoun was the catalyst, of course.

When they went into Saliha's bedroom, Izz Allah began stuttering and stammering, but she just gave him an icy look that froze his hands: 'After you have a son, you can do whatever you want. Until then, not another word. Now go to your bedroom, you two.' They withdrew, holding onto each other for support and fighting back their disappointment, almost breaking out in laughter.

It took three years of carrots, sticks, abnegation and chafing under the strictures of Saliha's regime, for the first signs of pregnancy to appear. Saliha was fed up with this girl, who needed re-raising from the start, and began to worry she'd made a bad choice, but her patience finally paid off and then she even let up a little bit and recalled the story of al-Bunni and the bird curse on her insomniac nights. Futoun's motherly instincts caused her to give into Saliha's indomitable strength. She kept to her south-facing bedroom, prevented from receiving friends. The tyrannical woman's rules were clear and they applied equally to her husband, the descendant of al-Bunni, who was confined to the parlour; he was more like a figment of the imagination and no one paid much attention to him. He was only allowed to attend to the fig orchard, to harvest, and to make prognostications about the intentions of the clouds: would they rain heavily this year or would they head westward to the Mountain of the Bearded Shaykh?

Saliha, who'd crushed her own husband under her thumb, understood that if he didn't have a system and priorities and a job to do, the family would fall apart, which was why she'd imposed her tough regime on everyone. Even her poor daughter Rahma, who'd been taken out of the second grade to look after her brother, when her job was over, when Izz Allah had finally escaped death, was surprised to find herself consigned to the ranks of the celibate. She ascended to the first echelons, when her mother turned away the only suitor who'd ever dared to ask to marry her:

'We don't have any daughters for marrying.'

The excuse that was given was that the boy's father had collaborated with the French. Anyone who even considered Rahma had to make allowances for her fearsome mother and her uncanny memory of all the mountain region's lineages and ancestral foibles. None of the potential daredevil suitors could pretend to be free of any disgraces committed by their forefathers and which were preserved in her unholy memory.

It was true that the other three daughters had miraculously managed to escape spinsterhood, but Saliha gave her son-in-laws more than enough grief and humiliation as she revealed to them every false step on their family trees. When Saliha finally realised that things could never move forward this way, she loosened her prohibitive conditions, but Rahma had already been to the mountaintop of her solitude and decided to carry out the mission that had been chosen for her: she vowed to look after her brother and his family. 'I don't want to get married', she told her mother. 'I want to help raise my brother's children.'

Thus Rahma exited the domain of categories. She lived on as little as possible. She made her living from her Singer sewing machine, gave her love to the animals and hens, and shared her capacity to rear with everyone in a ritual that bordered on the sacred. Rahma never changed. She stayed in the same clothes for decades, kept to her old familiar routine to this very day, her same gentle spirit, rather like a saint. She never left the environs of Sarmada, an area of twenty square kilometres, except for twice in her entire life. Once to work as a maid in Beirut like a lot of other girls from the mountains during the unification with Egypt, when the country was plagued by drought, locusts and the secret police, and the population was subject to poverty and hard times, worse than anything the mountains had never seen before in their entire history.

She went to Beirut, but she couldn't remember anything about it except for how she'd broken the china. She cried for hours and told the Beiruti lady of the house, 'I wish it was my hand that broke, ma'am, and not your china!' The woman didn't say anything, she just turned and walked away. Not three seconds had passed before the flutter of pity felt for teary-eyed Rahma had worn off; this girl had come from the south of Syria, along with dozens of other girls under the age of seventeen from the Druze and Alawite Mountains to work as servants in Beirut's mansions and villas. To help their folks, tormented by drought and Nasser's informants, which was the only idea that took root in Syria after the catastrophe of unification was over.

These were the people who'd become famous for their boundless generosity in the days when the Ottoman tyranny drafted the people either into the military or hard labour and they were besieged by Janissaries and locusts. God was angry at the Levant. The mountains remained, thriving and fawned over by the Turks. They continued to enjoy the freedom to shelter those who asked for protection from Ottoman tyranny, and thus the mountains turned into a thorn in the side of the Sublime Porte and the focus of a constant and merciless hand-wringing. They spread rumours about the people who lived there – what godless heretics they were. And their enemies even got bribe-inclined shaykhs to issue *fatwas* excluding the Druze from the communities of protected minorities and making it a sin to eat or drink with the Druze. They wanted to tie the area up in a sectarian conflict to disturb the cosy hospitality afforded to refugees and fugitives from the rotten justice of the Turks.

When famine struck the Levant, the parlours of the mountain houses welcomed people fleeing from Lebanon, Jordan, Palestine, the Hejaz and other parts of Syria. They fed and clothed them, and shared all that they had with those who'd come to the mountains seeking help. They opened their doors to people regardless of sect and offered safety, food and solace. The mountain region saved more than 50,000 refugees from famine, disease and Janissary corps impressments. But eventually those memories were squeezed out because Sarmada, like the rest of the mountain villages, only ever talked about the tragedies that befell them. They never bragged or patted themselves on the back, and everything was forgotten after independence.

The mountains gave up 2,231 martyrs, many of whom were killed defending Damascus, Hama, Idlib, Talkalakh, the Beqaa, the Hauran, Marjayoun and Rashaya al-Wadi, while the rest of Syria combined only gave up 1,800 martyrs in the struggle for independence. After independence was won, the leader of the revolution, who was a son of the mountains, simply returned to his fields to eat from his own harvest and to wear what he wove himself. He returned home, renouncing power and politics, and opened his parlour up to anyone in need.

So how then could it have happened that someone who'd helped to write the history of his country with his own blood and toil should have to watch as some of his daughters found nothing for their futures except to go to Beirut and work as maids? When they asked Sultan Pasha al-Atrash what he thought about the government of independence, he had only one thing to say: 'It makes you long for the days of the French occupation.'

Rahma had shouted with the crowd of villagers on the border of Sarmada for hours when Nasser came to visit the mountain region in 1960:

Hey Gamal,
look, we said,
you can take our men,
but give us bread.

She'd been expecting the inspiring leader to do more for the people, who believed so earnestly in him and his vision.

Nasser waved to the crowds, and he did actually take the men, but to prison. And his corrupt regime managed to leverage the sons of revolution's isolation and poverty to get them to send their daughters to Beirut to work as maids, and they brought drought and informants, but the bread never came.

Saliha, who'd only very reluctantly agreed to let Rahma go work in the mansion of a well-off relative, didn't sleep for an entire week and then she made up her mind. She went there herself, broke into the mansion – not giving a damn whose home it was – and dragged Rahma back to Sarmada. It was the first time in her life that she had allowed her affection to show in public and she squeezed her daughter tightly against her chest. She brought out a few gold lire she'd been saving up for times like those and supported the family until the drought passed.

The second time Rahma left Sarmada, she disappeared for twenty days and no one had a clue where she'd gone to, but then she just turned up again with a self assured smile and a vague cag-iness about where she'd been that she never disclosed. The thing no one knew was that she'd gone to return something to Hamza's family that her father had entrusted to her; it was something he'd been given on the day of the famous battle of Musayfara. Hamza al-Yusuf and five of his sons were flag-bearers that day and they were all martyred in battle. Before Muhanna breathed his last in the arms of his friend Shaheen, Rahma's father, he gave him a rosary and a silver ring with a precious stone, and asked him to give them to his wife. Shaheen was wounded in the battle and fled from the mountains to Wadi Sirhan with a group of fight-ers who rejected any talk of amnesty and remained there for ten years until the national government took power. Only then did he return, and with his companions searched everywhere for his comrade's widow, but he failed to find any trace of her, so he held onto the rosary and ring and charged Rahma with returning them to their rightful owner. And that's exactly what she did, although she kept the secret to herself. She travelled to the Eastern District and found his wife Mudallala and her son Hamza, whom she'd named after his martyred father. Rahma gave her what she'd come to give her and returned home.

Rahma's twenty-day disappearance gripped Sarmada and a whole saga's worth of stories were woven around her absence. No one could even bring themselves to think that Rahma had gone to meet a man, and so Sarmada greeted her absence with consternation and it kicked their imagination into overdrive. The disappearance of a woman with such a great, though unnoticed, presence, unless caused by her death, is bound to cause a disturbance in the lives of her fellow humans, and the animals and even the plants around her. But the last person to see her could tell that she'd followed al-Bunni's old trail and disappeared.

When she returned, life filled the house and questions filled their eyes. The smell of manure wafted off the burning cowchips. The troughs of the bay cow and the donkey were filled with moist grass and brittle straw, and the boughs were trimmed on the giant mulberry tree, which had been planted back in 1927 when the foundation of the house was laid by Abu Aboud al-Dhib, the most famous builder in the whole of the western district and the father of Aboud Scatterbrains, who would die of a heart attack caused by intense joy when Farida agreed to marry him.

The floor of the house was made from salvaged Roman bricks that dated back two millennia. Some of them still bore the markings of the ancient temples and there was the figure of an ancient Roman deity looking out from the mortar where they made their kibbeh. Out in front of the house, there was a vegetable patch, in the centre of which stood the young mulberry tree. They used to raise silkworm larvae on its leaves in the first half of the century before synthetic silk infiltrated the market and wiped out the venerable trade. Her every morning began with the call to the dawn prayer coming from the direction of the Muslim village of Busur al-Hareer and then she'd put on her gauzy headscarf, repeat the name of God a few times, mutter some prayers, and get up to attend to her chores. She let the lambs out and fed the cow. A lamb would butt her playfully and she'd slap his face in jest: 'Just wait for the Feast of the Sacrifice, my little kebab. Please God make its tail big and fat for our sake!'

She picked up the pace and lit a fire in the stove: 'Dear Lord, the dough snuck up on me! It's already risen.' And then she began to bake her delicious rounds of bread on those dewy mornings.

Singing, bleating, and the music of life filled the air as the day broke and the bread browned. She went over to the cow and washed its udders, and then the sound of milk crashing in the pan could be heard along with her mumbled blessings and 'in the name of God's ...'. She swept the floors of the house, let the grazing animals out to graze, and all the while kept up her constant conversation with the many animals.

The wait for rain had gathered all the children together to begin the rites of rain-summoning: they carried ceramic dishes from house to house and they were joined only by widows whose prayers were heard more loudly in the highest heaven than the prayers of married women, and they repeated:

'O mother of torrents, inundate us!
At the Shaykh's house, accommodate us!
If it weren't for him, you'd still await us!
He's always happy and willing to fete us!'

And they followed that with another poem:

'O mother of torrents, O Salman,
Water our thirsty plants!
O mother of torrents, O Shibli,
Water the plants till they're dribbly.
O mother of torrents, O Dayim,

Water our plants till they're slimed.'

Only a few days later, the downpour arrived.

When the rain came, out came the wild radish and gundelia and cockscombs and mushrooms and camomile and mallow and chicory. And the harmony of the restrained, not very green, but very rich place was recalibrated for no man wronged nature and nature was never stingy toward man. Rahma herself was part of this symbiotic system, of the trace of goodness running through the place, because her unique smile was key to getting the rams ready for slaughter. It almost made her smile to watch the cycle of nature unfold, to see the old Torah rituals repeated on the day of Abraham's son's sacrifice. The ram bleated with extraordinary resignation as she went up to it and wiped its face, looking deep into its eyes, confirming the firm bond between the two despite their contradictory fates: the gleaming calm in the eye of the sheep and Rahma, who could see straight through into the heart of things and understood in her expansive soul the forces of nature and its awesome cycles. The only time she found she couldn't look into an animal's eyes was the day Amira fell to the ground after the men of the village had failed to lure her down from the edge of the cliff, and yet still she sharpened the cleavers and handed them to the men and watched as the beloved cow fell to its death.

'Izz Allah's my father and Futoun bint Jabir's my mother. I was raised by my aunt Rahma and I'm the last in the al-Rayyash family line.'

Saloum looked into her eyes and continued: 'Buthayna, I know a lot of what I'm saying sounds like mumbo jumbo, but I wanted you to hear it all before we get married.'

Evening had settled over Sarmada and an agreeable silence washed over them as they sat on the roof of the house. She looked at him through a veil of darkness pierced by the rays of the setting sun as he faintly squirmed. She had only one thing to say: 'When are we leaving?' He couldn't believe what he'd heard! He was so happy and all he wanted was to hug her and carry her and fly away with her. She stopped him, gently: 'There'll be time for that soon enough.'

Two weeks later, in the summer of 1979, they were married and they left in September for the Emirates where he was to begin work as a teacher on assignment there. They had a small party with some relatives and Buthayna told Farida she wanted her to hold on to the house keys for her: 'If I don't come back in fifteen years, sell the house and donate the money in the memory of my mother and brothers.' She left her a declaration of power of attorney and the deed to the house to see to things. She wanted to leave and she didn't want to take any desire to return with her, so she scrubbed Sarmada clean of any trace of herself, or to quote: she did all that so she could try to bury her memories, as if it were some kind of funeral that was going to help her prepare for her new life. The night before they left, a flustered Farida paid her a visit. 'Beware of al-Rayyash's son. He might not be able to produce an heir.'

'If it's my fate, then he'll come,' said Buthayna as teary-eyed Bulkhayr stood by the door, his heart experiencing its first ever loss, and the one it would never get over.

In addition to Buthayna's hasty marriage to Saloum al-Rayyash, her departure for the Gulf, and the abrupt cancellation of the molasses lessons, Bulkhayr also came down with the measles. He was laid up sick in bed, his body consumed by fever with his skin attacked by a red rash; it broke Farida's heart to see him like that. She stayed up three nights in a row, preparing solutions and herbs, changing his cool compresses, listening as he deliriously recounted memories of the grape molasses and his auntie Buthayna, his heart broken, inconsolable and confused. Despite all her talents, Farida failed to find a combination of herbs that could drive the fever out of his young body and her old fears began to slip back in through the pores of her mind and demolish her fragile sense of security. The only thing that helped to hold her fears slightly at bay was Bulkhayr's recovery, although profound sadness still caused his eyes to glaze over, and he was morose and silent. His beautiful smile disappeared as did his former life-loving vigour. Most of the time he sat there withdrawn with his thoughts elsewhere.

His days passed calmly by in the midst of all the amazing and frightening changes taking place in Sarmada: the arrival of electricity, the asphalted roads and the transformed look of the place. All it took was one government initiative and the roads of a new life broke through the desolate tracts of basalt and boulders, and electricity began to stretch its way to the towns and villages. Something was changing in that village as it stood on the brink of new expectations that broke in on it forcibly, as all its ancient features faded and finally disappeared. It was as if one final round of governmental punishment had managed to infiltrate its innocence, had begun to tame the place and strip it of its long-standing and deep-rooted character.

The villagers were waiting for new things to take their place in their new lives, but they could never anticipate how great that change or transformation would be for the new patterns of life that arrived like another world. They received a surprise visit from the regional police who gathered up all the weapons in Sarmada and who would later take anyone carrying an unlicensed weapon to the infamous Tadmor prison, which would become permanently branded in the Syrian memory as the place where people were subjected to terror and the crushing of lives. The government, which remained on the outside, planted eyes and spies, and people with nice handwriting who liked to try to outdo one another with the reports they wrote about the odd vagabond or transient vagrant, which they rounded up and sent off to the various branches of the secret police. There they and their write-ups would be processed at dawn and escorted down into the chambers of torture and intimidation.

Even one of the police chiefs, who'd finished his service in the mountain region and was being transferred to a different district, said jokingly during a farewell party that the people of the mountain were compelled to throw for him, 'The mountains don't even need the secret police or any security force, really.' When they asked him what he meant, he explained gloatingly, 'Because people with good handwriting' (a euphemism for informants) 'are everywhere – God be praised. The government doesn't even have to bother hiring spies, you people do all the work yourselves!' All the mountain elites laughed disingenuously, flattering the corruptest one of all.

The village shaykhs could see the transformations were killing off their authority, which was already in freefall, so they began to warn the people about the signs of the end times and the apocalypse, and Shaykh Shaheen, who'd inherited the head shaykhship from Shaykh Mumps – Shaykh Farouq – laboured tirelessly to decipher the symbols in the Epistles of Wisdom. After a long period of seclusion, he made an announcement to the villagers: 'We are in the middle of the phase of exposure. This is the last phase of life. The resurrection draws near. There can be no doubting it, for it is said that a millennium shall pass, and not two, and that means that the resurrection will take place before we reach the year 2000.'

A smart alec retorted: 'That's all fine, Shaykh, but do the Epistles of Wisdom work on AD time or AH time?' Shaykh Shaheen stormed off, muttering strange words past a mocking crowd of open-minded youths.

The people of Sarmada felt that they could no longer remain the masters of their own lives, that the future would change everything, and that they simply had to go along with it, to abandon 300 years of independence, chivalry and an innocent way of life. They were undefeatable when it came to repelling clearly identified, hostile outsiders who intruded on their lives, but a government as secretive as this one, didn't even stir up the slightest dust.

Bulkhayr and his only friend Fayyad watched what was happening around them with disbelief. Suddenly they heard a thundering sound: 'Explosion! Run!' Now that the basalt boulders had been laid with dynamite, the children shouted that sentence over and over again that autumn and the windows rattled.

Then electricity poles were erected at regular intervals alongside the first asphalt road to cut between the houses of the village and connect them to the main road that travelled between the mountains and the outside world. The roar and racket of the huge machine that crushed the rocks and smoothed the asphalted road startled the donkeys and grazing animals as it approached and all of Sarmada, every last soul, went out to watch the huge iron beast level the earth. When Fayyad asked, 'What's that machine called?', one of the workers answered haughtily.

'It's a steamroller.'

Something peculiar happened to the steamroller just two weeks later: all its screws and anything else that could be removed were stripped off and it was just abandoned there. It remained as a massive, metal shell squatting in the middle of Sarmada for twenty years until the government finally decided to remove the wreck and repair it.

Bulkhayr just barely passed first grade and ran aground in the second, causing a great deal of bewilderment and frustration. His teacher, Ibtisam, had predicted a bright future for him at first, and had gone so far as to record it in her grade book, but the outlook soon deteriorated and he became the laziest student of all. The great void – or rather the crushing abyss – that the molasses-tutor had left behind her caused him to lose any interest he'd once had in school. The boy who'd once dazzled his teachers and classmates with his enviable reading and writing skills and his precocious vocabulary suddenly lost his passion and reduced his teacher to a temporary period of soul-searching: how could this boy, who'd been near genius-speed at learning, memorising and arithmetic, forget everything so quickly and without any forewarning? She blamed herself for pronouncing him gifted too hastily – for being taken in – and then cured his scholastic deterioration with that old Syrian standby: she sent him to the back of the class. There he shared a desk with the most hopeless student ever to enter Sarmada elementary, Fayyad al-Hadi, and the two of them would sit there, paying no attention to the reading and its boring characters like Basem, Rabab, and Hamid the industrious farmer, or to the Baath-scout cheers, or to the solemn celebrations of Our Father the Leader and the Mighty Baath, or to the curses hurled at Camp David and the Arab collaborators, and the rest of the rubbish they stuffed into the malleable minds of children. Later they would learn to revile the government of Iraq and its bloodthirsty leader, though the naïve children couldn't understand why people would say such things about a sister-nation like Iraq that was ruled by the same Baath party, or how it could be worse than Israel as their teacher insisted.

Of course, Bulkhayr and Fayyad couldn't give a damn about all that crap, and they didn't even bother to move their lips or pens as they were meant to. They had better things to do – things that were more important to them than songs, revolutionary cheers, reading lessons and the revolting things they had to memorise. Bulkhayr was still suffering from a painful loss and Fayyad from run-away fantasies of leaving Sarmada and going to Beirut, the city of his dreams and desires.

Workers shouting in warning: 'Explosion! Run!' shook Fayyad al-Hadi from his overpowering daydreams. His friend Bulkhayr was his only consolation. Bulkhayr, who was himself still tormented by the bitter terror of love that Sarmada never stopped drowning him in. All the men and most of the women in the village were tender and forgiving. They showered him with gifts and attention but their exaggerated love felt almost clammy. Fayyad's situation was the complete opposite: for him, it was unanimous rejection, denial and rebuke. But the two boys discovered together that cloying love and blind hate had united them in a unique friendship.

They felt that some mysterious common denominator linked their two destinies so they spent every day of their dull childhood together and refused to let anyone else tag along, except on adventures. They impatiently waited for Farida to deliver what she'd promised Bulkhayr: a black and white Syronix television. The appointed day finally came and a big truck pulled up and dropped off three bewildering contraptions. Bulkhayr spent three whole days asking his mother questions like:

'Is that the refrigerator?'

'No, my love. That's the washing machine.'

'Is that the television?'

'No, dearest. That's the refrigerator.'

Until Saeed the blacksmith, who'd become an electrician in the meanwhile, came over to Farida's house and connected them to the grid. And on that same Thursday evening in the spring of 1980, an antenna went up on the roof of the shed and after his mother had gone to the majlis for Thursday prayers, Bulkhayr and his friend watched the Egyptian film *Not Twenty and Already in Love* on Israeli Television's Arabic hour. As the film ended, a one-sided love story began starring Fayyad and Yusra, the leading lady, and from that day forth, she swept through his life like a hurricane. He was instantly infatuated and even the direction of his dreams changed from Beirut to Cairo! He went on to cut out all her photos and stories about her from magazines and newspapers, to see her films, and to hang on her every word, her every whisper. He even used to close his eyes during certain scenes because he couldn't stand to see her smothered by an actor's kisses.

As they entered sixth grade, Fayyad was considerably older than the rest of the students because he'd started school a year late and failed the first grade as well as the second where he'd met Bulkhayr. Mr Zaydoun, the school principal, cursed the idiotic idea of compulsory education and decided he'd simply pass the boy until they were finally rid of the jackass – his preferred name for Fayyad.

Of course, for Fayyad, school was nothing more than a place to sleep and hang out with Bulkhayr. He lived with his partially blind grandmother and worked from time to time with Saeed the blacksmith, and later electrician, in his shop. The bright light of the welder had damaged Fayyad's eyes so he now had trouble making things out at night. He spent his precious free time with Bulkhayr, constantly coming up with new ways to annoy Sarmada, although it always ended with the villagers overlooking Bulkhayr's involvement and taking out all their anger on Fayyad.

They went on walks every day through the rocky tracts, fantasising about running away together to somewhere some day: Bulkhayr to Damascus and his longed-for dream and Fayyad to his sweetheart Yusra in Cairo. In that hopeless place, their friendship deepened, as did their thirst for revenge against the tyrannical school principal and his punishments. They were just on the brink of puberty at that time. Zaydoun, the principal, was one of those who ate up everything the Baath put out and then got indigestion for it. His first child had Down Syndrome and his second was mentally retarded and it caused him to turn the school into a merciless military regime. All the elementary school students were frightened of him and he had spies who infiltrated among them and reported back to him – even during the summer holidays!

He forbade the children from swimming at either the western or the eastern ponds and he invented punishments for every student who got less than seven out of ten in their exams. The lazy students who failed to do their homework or did poorly in their exams had to queue up in front of his office so he could brand their supple cheeks with a marker: *Lazybones*. Instead of playing during recess, the lazy students were made to clean the toilets or they had the entire school laughing at them as they lined up in a ridiculously long single-file chain and marched around the sports pitch throughout the entire sports lesson or recess, led by none other than Fayyad al-Hadi. 'Train of lazies!' he'd bellow, pulling the others along, as they held on to one another's waists behind him and repeated: 'Choo choo!'

Zaydoun ran the local party and the 'Yellow' school, so called for the school's dingy colour, with a martial, 'take no prisoners' spirit, cursing the power that had sent him apes to teach instead of children. He even started railing against UNICEF of all things because it was an organisation specifically devoted to caring for children and he cursed it every morning along with everything else that had to do with kids. He used to beat the children sadistically: he'd rap their hands until they burned and he never hesitated to have them hoisted up and whip them on the soles of their feet, or to slap them, or squash them underfoot, especially during the Baath-scout classes where they were supposed to learn marching drills and the meaning of discipline. He planted the germ of loyalty to the pioneering party and Our Father the Leader in their little minds and woe to those children who couldn't get their heads around the proto-military manoeuvres or the right replies to the scout cheers that glorified the mighty Baath.

Over time, the two best friends got used to being lazy and the slur stained onto their cheeks didn't bother them anymore. They met ridicule with their own, doubled down and totally shameless, and if anything, it only added to their devilry. They used to dig up skulls out of the cemetery once they figured out they could sell them to Jawdat, the hopeless medical student. He paid them twenty lire per skull and then he sold them in Damascus for fifty. So the two of them became a pair of regular old grave-robbers. They used to steal electrical wires and make fully functioning toy cars out of them, which they then sold to the other kids, or else they'd work as lookouts for the guys hunting lost treasure among the valleys, stones and wasteland. They learnt how to set bird traps, how to make catapults and slingshots, and how to steal chickens out of coops. They were pros at marbles, at training the donkey foals to thresh, at collecting mushrooms and at making paper planes.

One day they got punished by Zaydoun and his colleague Mr Four-Eyes – their special name for the teacher otherwise known as Khalil the freak – a hard-line and humourless communist, who wore thick glasses. He was constantly disgusted by everything around him and never stopped ridiculing the two boys for being totally worthless and unserious. Khalil was the big intellectual whom the security forces had forbidden from teaching anything but elementary classes because they wanted to limit the influence of teachers with deviant political views. On the day the boys were punished, the two men were unanimous in their rage, though they each had their own reasons. They reprimanded Bulkhayr and Fayyad because the boys had gone and terrorised the entire village: they'd smeared themselves with black soot and dressed in sheep-skins – they were still half-naked – and walked around knocking on people's doors and shrieking at whoever answered. They didn't even think twice about going and scaring the two teachers after midnight and they capped off their insane night by scrawling mocking slogans onto the victory arch that hung over the entrance to the village. Next to where it said: 'One Arab Nation, One Eternal Mission', Fayyad climbed up and wrote: 'Principal Zaydoun and Mr Four-Eyes will suck you off for a kilo of limes.' They ended up writing that sentence all over the place: on the walls of the school, beside the main bus stop, on the walls of the party office and on either side of Poppy Bridge.

When the village woke up to that effrontery, the slogan began to circulate in whispered mocking as they secretly saluted whoever had written it. The whole of Sarmada was fed up with Zaydoun, who stuck his nose into every last thing. Sure, he'd planted trees around the village and done some good things, and he'd arranged for a bus link between Sarmada and the city, but he'd also forced the Baath on the docile village. He was the one who collected the memberships and made sure everyone attended the Monday meetings. He was always saying, 'The Baath comes first. Don't anyone think they're more important than the Baath. The Baath's more important than God Himself!' Because he had a close relationship with the secret police, and because he wrote precise reports for them about what was going on in the village, and because he paid bribes to those higher-up in the party and put on regular banquets for the mountain region's party leaders and political police, he'd been able to foil any attempts to push him out.

Khalil the communist, on the other hand, had cut himself off from the rest of the village after he'd discovered he was infertile and incapable of impregnating his wife, who decided that what she wanted was a divorce, but not because he couldn't make her pregnant, no, rather because he was always so miserable and so contemptuous of everyone and everything. He withdrew after the divorce. He didn't take part in any of the holidays or festivities anymore; it even got to the point where he began to resent his younger communist comrades. He looked down his nose at them to compensate for his inferiority complex and emasculation, and eventually, he became intractable, rancorous and intolerant; he was unable to forget let alone forgive the tiniest slight, and he even bore a grudge against one of his comrades who'd failed to return a greeting when he'd been lost in thought.

Khalil's sole accomplishment was a polemic he'd published on the class conflict between landowners and peasants, in addition to some poetry, which was boring but wholly engaged with the 'Big Issues' and copied the style of Socialist Realism from the writers of Moscow and the Soviet camp. The communists who were part of the government and the National Progressive Front had a lot to say about him as they usually did. After all, these were the people who'd agreed to become regime lackeys in exchange for access to the few cultural pulpits in the country like the Ministry of Culture and they accepted those jobs as a sort of bribe that sapped them of their revolutionary enthusiasm for change.

They were content to have the perks of the Writers Union, which was essentially a place where the intellectuals were kept, where they could bleat their slogans about resisting imperialism and the oppressive Zionist enemy while at the same time praising the rulers who'd taken a stand against liberty and liberation and instituted the harshest, most illegitimate, and most repressive regime in the history of the country, indeed in the history of the entire region.

They eventually reduced culture in Syria to one colour and shape, especially after the death, imprisonment and exile of the communists who'd refused to sell out so cheaply. Only a handful remained – all friends of Khalil – and they elevated whoever they felt like elevating and snootily cast out anyone who had trouble insinuating themselves into their little group and its gatherings.

The scabby leftist culture-claque needed to recruit someone from the mountain region so they could pretend to be anti-sectarian and plural-minded nationalists, and Khalil was exactly what they'd been looking for. They promptly proclaimed him the 'Neruda of Syria,' but the people of Sarmada, on the other hand, took great delight in the graffiti attacking the two most despised men in the village. As usual, they went easy on Bulkhayr and his punishment was limited to a verbal dressing down and six raps on the knuckles with the edge of a ruler, but Fayyad, well, now he was hauled up onto the cabinet and had his feet whipped like a war criminal until they swelled up. As you can well imagine, the punishment didn't put the boys off, it just made them more careful.

The boys spent their days wondering about the one question that plagued them constantly: how could they pass the hardest test of all? The one that would allow them to leave aside childish games and join Sarmada's gang of young men.

Before they could take the plunge and venture to where the older boys hung out, they had to undergo the ritual that marked the transition from childhood to young-manhood. It took place at the western pond where the last of the water in the valley all pooled in a large depression. There it would remain throughout the summer, making it the perfect place for the children to swim and play. Fayyad and Bulkhayr, who were both dying to join the village gang, would have to put on a show for the older boys, but when the time finally came, Fayyad had second thoughts about masturbating in front of all the other boys. They only had one chance to prove that they could ejaculate – that they'd become men – but if they failed, they'd be subject to endless bullying, so Fayyad decided he wouldn't take part. Bulkhayr stood by his friend and also refused to perform, though he had to fight back the rage he felt when they were subjected to Ramez Donkeyshit's jeering abuse – and yet he let them watch the induction ceremony of the other three boys who'd come to the pond all the same.

The pubescent boys stood in a row in front of the crowd and then the show began: they took off their trousers and sat down in a row on the bank of the brackish water and then as Ata the impish storyteller told them about his experiences with gypsy women, the boys began to play with their dainty bits. Ata repeated the same story, adding his constant embellishments, calling to mind how the gypsy woman smelt and how he attained the deepest depths of pleasure, sliding into a moist, velvety vagina and thrusting fever-ishly into her behind as the gypsy woman cried with delight. All those different details and many more he'd throw in. Every time he told the story, he added a few scenes he'd seen on Israeli televi-sion, which always broadcast 'erotica', although that was just what people called it, in truth they were just comedies, which didn't have the hot scenes edited out. The story grew only more passion-ate as the fists gripping the strained members shuttled and shook ever more fervidly, and the boys were lost in their own imagina-tions, horny and holding back moans, and then the older boys were suddenly cheering and their task was complete and that wide, new world they'd been dying to get into finally opened up and welcomed them.

Ata stood up and congratulated the boys, and then he per-formed the last rite. He cut the stem of a yellow-flowered plant called milk thistle and gave a few drops of the golden, alkaline sap to each boy and made him rub the stinging drops on his penis, to make it grow – so it was said – but actually only to make it swell, and to make the boys suffer days of unbearable pain, with tears in their eyes, but stupid proud smiles on their faces.

Bulkhayr tried to get Fayyad to go through with the performance because if he didn't prove to the older boys that he was able to ejaculate, he would never be allowed to join that other world, or get to go on trips to the brothels in Damascus with the gang, or accompany them on gypsy women raids, or listen to the adults' sex-soaked stories, or learn how to ride Ata's motorcycle for almost no money at all, and that he'd be just a boy for the rest of his life, forbidden from taking part in that other, unseen side of Sarmada. But Fayyad was scared. He told Bulkhayr that what had happened to Mamdouh the shopkeeper's son, Essam, had scared him and he was worried that it might happen to him, that he, too, might fail the test and that the older boys would then start to molest him and treat him as if he were a girl.

He was entirely right, of course: their burning passion had them raping farm animals and just waiting for someone they could penetrate like Essam. The only thing he could do – in the end – was dress himself in a hood and loose trousers and become a shaykh who never left the majlis, putting an end to his worldly life, and saving his arse too, because no one dared lay a hand on a young shaykh who was protected by the Holy Spirit, the five cosmic principles and God Himself!

Fayyad began testing his penis in private while looking at pictures of the actress Yusra because that small erection was his key to a greater world. Then Bulkhayr happened upon the solution when he discovered that the boys were also allowed to prove their manhood at Stone-deaf's terebinth tree.

'Do you want me to come with you?' he asked Fayyad.

'No, I'm going to go on my own. I'll tell you what happens later.'

From far away, Sarmada looks like it's stripping off its clothes after a warm summer day, getting ready to await another morning. My camera snaps wide shots, panning wide-frame over a landscape of seduction and mystery. Yes, I lived here once, but now it's as if I'm from somewhere else. The sleeping village offers its dreams up to my wakefulness and my wakefulness selects only what agrees with my memories to form a new space. I wondered whether Azza Tawfiq would ever see what I saw. Would she ever hear behind the sounds, or deep below them? I needed to speak to her. To ask her once more: Are you sure you're Hela Mansour?

If you want to really know yourself, you should stand stark naked in front of the mirror and get dressed very slowly; then leave. The last impression is the final impression. There's nothing deep down. Everything that happens rises up to the surface and is then spun off into new words. You just have to know how to gather them all. Learn how to write them down. Anyone who says we have to take advantage of time belongs to the machinery of work in contemporary life. To take advantage of time is to take advantage of others. Here in Sarmada, I discovered that time has no value. Only place can have value. Finding the right place: that's our precious mission. Time, we can't do anything about. Have I suddenly come down with a case of endings and over-withs? No, not yet.

Stone-deaf Siman will take over the story for the novel can end only in silence. Thus I, too, shall be silent now.

֍

The ancient tree stood in the quiet and tranquil wasteland and it was Stone-deaf Siman who'd discovered that the tree provided an incomparable means of proving manhood. The tree became a site of pilgrimage: fertility-seekers flocked to it from all across the country and picked its leaves, which they would steep along with camomile, rosemary and colocynth and when they drank the resulting tea, it would increase their fertility.

Fayyad put his fate in the hands of the blessed tree, which people said was actually just a woman of immense sexual appetite, profoundly lustful and debauched. She was never satisfied, one time she even slept with a whole division of the Nabatean army without so much as blinking. She lived in this same spot more than 2100 years ago, an Ishtarite woman with divine breasts and a voluptuous arse. She'd originally been abducted by a genie, but the king of the genies took a liking to her and he married her instead. He had to throw her out after a while, though, on account of how lascivious and fecund she was. She'd corrupted the entire underworld so she was sent back to the world of men with her fragrant vagina whose musk made humans swoon. She went on living like that, a slave to desire, until she was slain by a eunuch's axe and was transformed into this peculiar terebinth tree.

Stone-deaf Siman, who'd been the first to discover the tree's capabilities, planted a hedge of cypress trees all around it and began to work as the tree's pimp. He was probably the only tree pimp in the entire world as a matter of fact. Soon the tree's supple crevices and the hot resin bubbling up from its giant trunk, made it the village boys' favourite destination. To guard against surprise scratches, Siman had purchased a couple of kilos of off and putrid petroleum jelly and filled the suitable crevices. The shaykhs tried to spread rumours about him: that he'd been struck deaf and dumb once he'd started pimping out the tree and corrupting the young men in the village, but none of that seemed to matter to Fayyad as he proudly, and gaily, regaled his friend with a full report of his experience.

'I paid Stone-deaf Siman, the guy who guards the tree, three-quarters of a lira that I'd managed to save up in small coins, and then I dropped my trousers and took out my dick. I tested one of the holes with my finger. It was moist and sticky, so I stuck it in slowly and closed my eyes. It felt like the tree was blowing me. I wrapped my arms around it like it was Yusra, my sweetie. I could hear her whispering to me in Egyptian Arabic, she was saying,

"Yeah! That's it! You're driving me wild! Oh, baby, oh, Fayyad!" And then I busted inside the tree. The deaf guard was watching me the whole time and then when I finished, he walked over and made sure that I'd actually come inside the tree. Then he gave me a thumbs up, like he was saying "Mission Accomplished!"'

Bulkhayr laughed. 'The deaf guy's still giving you a thumbs up. The whole of Sarmada's going to start treating you like a man from now on.'

To make it official, Fayyad brought Stone-deaf Siman down to the spring with him. The boys had all gathered to find out the result from a few signs, and gestures of the head and hands, and then finally he gave Fayyad the all okay sign with two thumbs straight up, and they understood that Fayyad had made it into their world. At that point, loony Safwan taunted from the crowd: 'So what about you, Bulkhayr? Or is it still too soon for you?'

Without answering, he dropped his trousers, stripped off his underwear, and revealed two penises, each more than seven inches in length. Some of the boys ran from the terrifying sight, while others watched, jaws gaping, as Bulkhayr wanked one of them furiously until he came and then moved onto the next one, and finally completed the ritual of public masturbation in the midst of much cheering and singing from the others, who immediately elected him leader, despite his youth. He hadn't even turned twelve yet.

The school trip would change both of their lives forever. Principal Zaydoun had decided on a field trip to the famous shoe factory in the city and then to the top of the mountain to look out onto the miraculous meadow, where if you pour water on the road, it flows from low ground to high and where if the bus were parked at the bottom of the slope in neutral and the brakes were released, it would roll upward. The bemusing experience mystified the people of the mountains and visitors and as is to be expected, plenty of apochryphal stories were invented – creatively, but illogically – to explain the vexing phenomenon.

Of course, no one bothered to listen to the geologist as he tried to explain that it was all just an optical illusion and that the ground elevation wasn't as it seemed, and so the legendary explanations continued. Sarmada had a knack for, and sufficient practice at, taking something like that and turning it into a reason for faux-excitement, which spread from student to student as they awaited their upcoming trip.

Their itinerary took them from the meadow vista to the Roum Dam – an achievement of the 'blessed' revolution – and then onto the woods outside Kom al-Hisa, where they were going to have lunch. After lunch, they would visit the distillery where they made arak and wine, and finally end up at the shoe factory. The principal had contracted with Suhayb the bus driver to hire his big Scania bus for the trip.

What Bulkhayr and Fayyad didn't know, though, was that the principal had hatched a conspiracy to change the departure time from seven to half-past-six so that they would miss the trip. It was really Fayyad he was after because he didn't want that idiot ruining the trip with his mischief. A half hour before the journey was scheduled to begin, the principal gave the head scout boys and the bus driver strict orders not to let that lazy waste of space onto the bus under any circumstances. He wanted to make it look like it was all the students' idea: 'Do you lot want Fayyad coming on your trip?'

'No, sir!' answered one of the students who'd had a taste of the troublemaker's fist before. He was joined by the others, who were caught up in the thrill of the exclusion and the validation of their principal's smile, which they only saw once every few months. The whole group had been turned against Fayyad and they were feeling pretty proud and pleased with themselves, as well as obviously being quite surprised that their legendarily heartless principal was scheming with them, bucking them up even, and that he'd promised them an unforgettable school trip on the sole condition that the little miscreant be left out.

'Don't worry about it, sir. We'll see to it he never gets on the bus.'

'It's all up to you', said the wicked principal. 'You lot need to make a decision: do you want him on the trip or not? It's not my problem.'

They listened so closely that the morning drowsiness was wiped from their eyes, and then they divided up the positions themselves and one of them armed himself with the principal's cane. Two of them hung onto the back staircase to fight off any attempts to latch onto their long-awaited journey and the biggest and best kickers stood by the door to keep him from getting onboard under any circumstances. As the bus was about to set off, Bulkhayr and Fayyad appeared in the distance, out from behind the ruined steamroller that squatted in the middle of the village, and they began to sprint as quickly as they could. Bulkhayr got to the door first and the students who'd been appointed as guards grabbed him and pulled him onto the bus. But when Fayyad reached out, expecting to get the same help, he got whacked on the head with the principal's cane and he had no idea why. He backed off and tried to climb up the back staircase but they kicked him away and he stumbled, falling into the thorny bushes alongside the asphalt road, which looked to him like a black snake swallowing the bus up until all he could see was the sooty exhaust and that, too, began to dissipate. In the midst of a resoundingly silent morning, pierced only by his scattered, wrenching sobs, he stood there and wept in the brittle emptiness. He implored them with futile cries, but the speed of the bus and the ecstasy of their principal's complicity had made them into cruel and frantic little brutes. They stuck their heads out of the bus windows and pointed and gestured rudely, mocking the cry-baby who was running after them. Bulkhayr tried to stop them, but he got a punch to the face and a bloody nose for his trouble. He wanted to get off and he begged Suhayb to stop the bus, but there was no point. So then he started cursing at the students and trying to push past them to the back door, hoping to jump out and run back to his friend, but they held him back and knocked him down to the ground, where they kept him until the bus was far enough away, ignoring all his taunts and threats. The principal, meanwhile, was busy chatting to Ms Camellia, reeling off his really quite impressive track-record of imposing discipline on the students and the village at large, while she, for her part, tried to fake a bland smile as she wondered just how she'd managed to forget her maxi-pads on the counter at home and hid any signs of the abdominal cramps that accompanied her period, which had come that very morning and taken her by surprise.

The only available outlet for Fayyad's vengeance was the flag that flew high above the school so he tore it to shreds in a blind rage. After he'd returned, panting from his failed attempt to catch up with the bus, he sat down against the wall of the school, fighting back the tears that lit a fire in his heart and left him cursing the moment he'd ever been born into that shitty little village. He caught sight of the slack flag – the only thing moving he could see – and so he climbed up to the roof of the school and knocked down the flagpole, and then he began rabidly ripping the flag apart.

This was the flag that had greeted him every morning for eight years. The flag he'd revered. He used to think that saluting the flag was a duty, that it wasn't even negotiable on chilly or frozen mornings, irrespective of stomach-aches or stuffed noses. He'd always felt a special affection for that piece of cloth. Not saluting it was unthinkable – an act of treason beyond the pale. It was exactly like the Baath party slogans he'd memorised and taken to heart, even though he didn't understand a word of them. The teacher who stood in front of the students and pierced the disciplinary air with his booming voice told them that they were being called on to help build one grand and unified Arab socialist society and to defend it, and Fayyad would raise his right hand as if swearing an oath – proud that his own husky voice was loudest of all. Tearing up the thing he'd loved most at the school was like taking revenge against all those brutal years and it marked the end of a childhood that had been rather late in ending.

Back on the bus, the students danced with the glee of a mission accomplished, but their joyous racket was beginning to annoy the principal, who, after all, was trying to have a conversation with the new female teacher. He interrupted himself to shout at them and thereby regain some of the dignity he'd traded away that morning. The students all returned to their seats and only Bulkhayr was left, raving and cursing, not giving a damn about the principal's authority. Bulkhayr sprung to his feet and punched the boy who'd punched him and the one who'd thrown him down on the ground. The one who'd covered his mouth and held him down got kicked in the balls. Principal Zaydoun was livid and he couldn't control his tongue as he unleashed a torrent of abuse on troublemaking Bulkhayr, who would later come to see that moment as a fork in the road of his life.

'Sit down, you little bastard! You pathetic son of a whore, you don't even know who your own father is, and now you want to start acting tough and making threats. Trust me, you better sit the fuck down before it's too late.'

There was a heavy silence followed by giggling and sniggering from the students who couldn't believe they'd just heard those words come out of their principal's mouth. Then it was absolute pandemonium as Bulkhayr flew off the handle: he threw himself onto the bus driver and tried to wriggle his way into the driver's seat, so the driver was forced to stop the bus. The principal literally kicked the boy off the bus and then they continued on their exciting educational journey.

Bulkhayr was covered in dust. The bus let out a cutting honk as it carried on into the distance and the despondent boy turned back. He was only a few kilometres from Sarmada, but it felt so far away he thought he'd never get back and he desperately wished there was somewhere else besides that wretched little village where he could go and seek permanent refuge. His head began to fill with worrying fantasies, but they were soon interrupted by a military tractor-trailer hauling a broken-down tank, or perhaps it was an army truck with the sides torn off. The air seemed to pulse with a clamour and dingy smoke that he breathed in quickly. His memory, meanwhile, was busy gathering up every last hushed whisper, every suppressed wink, and arraying them in an appalling picture of the truth: he honestly didn't know who his father was. He was a bastard, and his mother was just a whore, and everybody in the mountain region knew it, everyone but him. All that love and good feeling he got from everyone in Sarmada was only because all the villagers thought he might be related to them.

As Fayyad was busy tearing the flag atop the school to shreds, Bulkhayr scratched through the veil that'd been wrapped tightly around his eyes and watched as his world began to fall apart. He reached the shed after two hours of dejected walking and Farida was surprised to see him home so soon. She sent away the patient, who'd come looking for help with flatulence and intestinal bloating, and wiped her hands on a white rag. He was filthy and his face looked ill with the poison of unvarnished truth. Her heart began to beat frenetically, her hands trembled and a bitter-tasting distress consumed her. He simply stood in front of her and stared straight into her eyes. Then clenching his fists, he asked a question that she could never answer: 'Who's my father?'

'What's wrong, my love? What happened?' she asked; his pointed question had nearly reduced her to tears. He'd finally found out, but she wasn't ready for that yet. She thought there was still time before she'd have to come clean.

'Who is he? Tell me who he is.'

'What's wrong, dear. Tell me what's the matter?'

'Answer me,' he said, cutting her off. 'How many times are you going to make me ask you? Give me an answer: who is my father?'

His insistence caught her throat and she thought back over all the houses in the village; every memory a pin-prick. She wanted to slap him, or maybe hug him, but the only thing she could bring herself to do was to grab the broom, pour some water out onto the ground, and begin to sweep the porch, submitting helplessly to the tears that overwhelmed her. He was still standing there, looking as if he'd aged ten years in an instant. The place grew silent, the sounds in the distance died out first, followed by the rustling in the trees. The village was still; he couldn't even hear the broom sweeping against the ground anymore. The only thing that remained was a buzzing, which appeared yellow-coloured somehow; the sound itself seemed yellowed and it surrounded him. He went into his bedroom and shut the door behind him.

The next morning, he was still clothed in that yellow buzzing. He couldn't hear the police cars that came to take Fayyad away after they'd been tipped off by Principal Zaydoun. He'd worried that the destruction of the flag had been the work of more than one culprit, and he even had to defend himself against some of the villagers who attacked him for being so underhanded and manipulative. Kalashnikov-wielding forces dressed in uniforms with stripes and shiny medals stormed into Fayyad's bedroom and dragged him away to the investigations bureau as if he were a war criminal or something.

He returned to the village nine weeks later to find that Bulkhayr had regained his sense of hearing, but that he could no longer see the colour yellow; he could only hear it. Bulkhayr came to see him at his grandmother's house. They sat across from each other as his nearly blind grandmother cried tears of joy and got up to bring them something to eat. Fayyad looked broken – as if he'd be broken forever and his spirit simply couldn't be fixed. Bulkhayr wasn't able to find any words of consolation – not for his friend, or for himself –and so he left him wordlessly, alone in his despair, and he wasn't at all surprised when Fayyad ran away a few days later. No one heard from him after that. Not a single message came for twenty years, not until 2006.

Everyone was celebrating the birth of 'A New Middle East', but it was born seriously deformed. In Iraq, death was serving up cheap daily specials, and Lebanon, the only Arab democracy, was a running joke. Who killed Hariri? It was just another question to add to the long list of history's unsolved cases, which stretched all the way back to the Caliph Uthman and his tunic. The 2006 War on Lebanon had left everyone in a difficult position because the winner hadn't really won, and the loser hadn't really lost. But it was especially bad for Sarmada, which watched Fayyad al-Hadi on their television screens returning from Lebanon after the war, reaching the border, and then the village itself. He'd come back from the depths of some faint, forgotten past. The collective memory of the village kicked into gear and the details reappeared instantly; he became the talk of the town and everyone remembered his name, and remembered to say a prayer of mercy for his poor grandmother who'd died cold and alone. They organised a grand homecoming for him with songs and ululations and festivities and the kind of high-brow, pulpit poetry you sometimes get. Everyone talked about him as if he'd been a close friend. His old principal – who'd been appointed mayor – praised him for his heroism and selfless devotion to his village, even as a child, and he mentioned how the boy had strived and toiled from earliest youth, and he explained that he took personal pride – the principal, that is – in having taught the boy about dignity and patriotism.

But to tell the truth, Fayyad didn't hear any of that. He was in a wooden box draped with the Syrian flag, lying in his lovely coffin. He'd been returned to the village as part of the very famous initiative between Israel and Hezbollah to exchange prisoners and the mortal remains of martyrs. He was taken to Lebanon first and then, after all those years, back to Sarmada. Today, his old elementary school in the village is named after him. There's a huge sign out front that reads 'Fayyad al-Hadi the Martyr Elementary School' and that same flag still flies over it.

৬৯

What with Fayyad running away to Lebanon, and his own punishing of his mother with silence and cutting himself off from
everyone in Sarmada, there was nothing left for Bulkhayr to do
but to take walks through the rocky wasteland and lock himself
away with Hamoud's books. He'd rooted them out of the attic. All
together, they amounted to about seventy books printed in the
1960s, faded and smelling of moths, and the leaves of some of the
books still hadn't been cut open, which meant they'd never been
read. He dusted them off and found they helped to take his mind
off things. The first book that stoked his appetite for reading was
Hemingway's *For Whom the Bell Tolls*. On the first page he found
a line in nice, clear handwriting: *From the library of Hamoud
al-Ayid*. He felt like erasing it, the name of his hypothetical father,
and writing his own name there instead. The sudden realisation
that his surname would never be al-Ayid made him shiver.

He devoured those seventy books in less than three months and
he decided he'd enrol in the middle school in the neighbouring
village. He didn't want to carry on at the school in Sarmada. He
couldn't bring himself to deal with any of the villagers anymore,
so he went to the middle school in the neighbouring village of
Minzar. He had to commute eight kilometres a day by foot
through the paths in the rocky wasteland, entertaining himself by
remembering the plots of the novels he'd read and contemplating
the forest of stone and all the different shapes it took.

He was silent at his new school, obstinately so, and quick-
tempered. When some of the older boys tried to test his mettle,
he easily bent one of their noses with a savage punch and they
all stayed out of his way after that. He sunk into the school
library and he didn't have any friends except for the few boys he
exchanged books with. One of them was a tall, borderline-dunce
whose father had a huge library and collected books merely for
decoration. The other kids were always trying to beat up the tall

boy and Bulkhayr stepped in to protect him from the older boys a couple of times.

Bulkhayr figured it was a gesture of thanks and loyalty when his new friend Faris al-Khateeb gave him the collected works of the poets al-Mutanabbi, Abu Ala al-Ma'arri and Abu Nuwas, out of which he memorised dozens of poems, but the truth of the matter was that Faris had seen the two willies dangling between Bulkhayr's legs in the toilets at school and something about that interested him, attracted him even. He decided to shower Bulkhayr with books because he knew that it was the only way to build a relationship with him, to grow close, and he even risked inviting him over to pick something out of the great big library at home for himself.

Bulkhayr leapt at the invitation. No one was home so Bulkhayr could take his time picking through the books which Faris' father, the high-ranking military officer, had collected to round out the prestigious accoutrements, which the well-off were meant to have. Every time Bulkhayr found a book that interested him, Faris would take it and stick it in a big bag until the bag was bursting with books. Bulkhayr couldn't help but feel a bit embarrassed about the excessive generosity afterward. They went and sat together in Faris' room and drank the tea Faris had prepared. Bulkhayr was uncomfortable; his friend was being a bit too fey, leaning a bit too close. Faris put on a cassette of the *Concierto de Aranjuez* and tried to put his hand between Bulkhayr's thighs. Bulkhayr stood up angrily and when Faris tried to get him to stay, he smacked him, knocking him to the ground, and stormed out, fuming and slamming the door behind him; partially rueing the bagful of books he'd had to leave behind.

In addition to ploughing through the books, he also went on long hikes through the wasteland where he spent hours upon hours examining the huge basalt stones and the wasteland wilderness, tracing the not-so-distant past when the people of the area finished off the forces of Ibrahim Pasha of Egypt in a battle in which whole divisions of Janissaries and French mercenaries were wiped out.

To him, the wide, wild wasteland was the most familiar place in the world, and he eventually started taking a small tent with him and a bag full of Hamoud's supplies, and even blazing a few short trails himself. That wilderness was where he thought and matured; it was where he learnt his silence and toughness, where he'd regained the peace and tranquillity he'd lost. His trips began lasting several days, which he'd spend lost in thought, communing with the rocks and the humped boulders and the august and immovable stones. Time meant nothing to him when he set his tent up and lit a fire beside flowing springs, or on the edge of the forest that lined the mountains, encircling the massive rock formations that lay just outside Sarmada. His hikes eventually took him deep into the heart of the Lajat. He'd sit for hours among strange ruins, enjoying the silence, contemplating the spirit of the basalt and all its shapes, its peculiar formations and figures, under a clear open sky and a bright sun, breathing in the pure air and all the scents of stone.

The wilderness of the wasteland was tamed in his contemplative mind and he began recording his first dense fragments in a special notebook, which he'd titled: *Transformations of Basalt and Sunlight*. It made him drunk with joy to record the lives of the rocks and their shapes, their relationship with the rain and the sun, their colours, how they changed over the hours of darkness and light, their breath as they soaked up the sun and swallowed the plants growing on them, how water collected on their surfaces after a downpour in little pools topped off by fleeting sparrows, or cicadas and other bugs come to stay. This seemed more perfect to him, these worlds opened up to the deep blue sky of day, pure and proud beneath the stars, which were like freckles on the sky at night.

In his notebook, he wrote about one rock that was pregnant with small pebbles. And with words, he painted a picture to show

how the earth drank the milky liquid of the stars from the mouth of the moon. He wrote about the foolish pebbles that wouldn't budge from beside a pool of water for more than 290 years and were absolutely covered in the droppings of thirsty sparrows. He recorded the whispers of silence in sentences that bulged with the ups-and-downs of the pock-marked face of a furious boulder. He absorbed the rocky insomnia and whispering solidity, he watched as the silt fermented and the pot-bellied boulder seemed to waltz. He committed the smells of the place to words, recording the nitrate-laden breezes in a poem he called 'A dictionary of zephyrs and abrasions'. He was overjoyed when he unlocked the language of basalt and its scent. He and they became one and then he could turn them into new words, which oozed energy and shine. His overpowering desire for discovery pushed him toward that magical spot in the mountains so he made up his mind to go and set up camp in Hebariyeh.

It was evening by the time he got there. Next to some ruins, he found a bearded man absorbed in prayer. The man had reclaimed a plot of about fifty square metres and ringed his garden with some strange stones he'd found; he also had a goat and a few chickens. The old man welcomed Bulkhayr and invited him to stay the night. Bulkhayr told the old man that he'd heard a great deal about Hebariyeh and that he wanted to find out the truth for himself. Was it really the ruins of Sodom and Gomorrah or just some settlement that'd been taken unawares by a volcano 5,000 years ago?

'Neither,' said the old man. 'Here, they used to make the graves out of leftover corpses. I bet they must've had to collect hundreds of corpses from all over the region. They heated them up with the rocks, at temperatures between 600 and 1000 degrees Celsius, so the bones mixed in with the rocks, as you can see. But no one has any idea why. Were they making sacrifices to the place? Or was it some primitive ritual having to do with ancient idols?'

Bulkhayr took a look around him. There were several huge stones with protrusions that were quite obviously joints, and palates and jaws complete with teeth. He could see fragments of bone, and crimson dirt, and lime, as well as stones inlaid with vertebrae and skulls. It was unlike anything he'd ever seen before, and this was the guy who'd memorised all the stones and different basalt shapes in the Lajat. But here were seven square kilometres of boulders, rocks and pebbles formed from the bones of humans and animals and from parts of trees that had been carbonised, and cooled, and preserved in strange and inexplicable shapes. He was totally taken with the place and he started leaping around like a maniac, looking, peering, poking, examining, recording, cheerfully collecting whatever small stones and scraps of metal he could get his hands on until darkness swallowed them up. The old man lit a fire and they kept each other company until the morning. Bulkhayr recited poems by Abu Nuwas and Abu Ala al-Ma'arri, as well as some four-liners he'd written himself about geological revelations, and the old man recited mystical poems by al-Hallaj, al-Suhrawardi and Ibn Arabi for him until daybreak. He woke up sluggishly and climbed to the top of a short hill and looked out over the crematory, the pit of massive stones. The layer of moss that had grown over the stones was soaked with dew. As the sun rose, the scene was transformed into a symphony of stunning colours and the first threads of dawn trickled out onto the freshly washed stones. The boy's forsaken heart was moved and – for the first time in his life – he understood that special, secret tingle the place gave off.

He stared at the rocks closely and saw that they possessed human features, faces. Some were crisp and distinct, others were disguised and dulled; some were lofty and fixed, others hidden and vague. They seemed pliant, and changing and sychronised as the dew began to gleam in a bath of light poured out from the fresh sun, and the desolation became a jungle bursting with colour and the buzzing and chirping of insects. It gave off the perfume of those millennia still stored up in that virginal, untamed place.

Places had their means of self-defence, too, he felt, just like primitive beings, and if he only listened and looked closely enough, he could liberate geography from its suspension. Place was no more than frozen time. And time was only flowing place. This was the paradox that gripped his heart and allowed him – for the briefest moment – to understand that anyone who came across this patch of earth was fated to resemble it, to bury his emotions beneath a stony, blood-red screen and to let them out only on mornings like this one.

He understood for the first time and forevermore that what kept the people here wasn't sectarian feeling or a sense of community, it was the spirit of the rocks, the virgin sentiments stored deep in the rugged wasteland, the secrets of the basalt. He felt the spirits of those whose corpses had been burned appear. He could hear them muttering, their footsteps. The dreams of people who'd performed their duty and returned to their rest appeared fleetingly before his eyes.

True nature can't just be some spindly plants, and forests and sand. It was rock and metal that had come together with unparalleled symmetry in order to put disorder straight. Nothing can be built if there's no solidity, nothing, not souls, not cities. The soul of a city is usually derived from the type of stones that are used to build it and relationships are formed based on the type of metal people use to shield themselves against nature.

As the sun rose up in the east, the dew dissipated in the driving heat. He didn't resist his conscience when it suggested that it was time to return to Sarmada. He didn't even think of the old man: whether he'd really been there or was a mere hallucination. He found a shady refuge from the midday heat and dozed off, watching as the history of the place played out before his eyes in a smooth rendition that led him – when he woke up – to the moral of the story: we're going backwards. We're walking back toward that first drop of primordial sperm. The future is nothing more than a past that's been achieved. That idea would gnaw at him for the rest of his life and lead him to venture into worlds no one had ever seen before.

Farida, who'd got used to his silence over the past four years and whose every attempt to get him to speak to her had failed, gave in to fate, as usual, and waited patiently to see what it had in store for her. She was nearing fifty, but her face was still vibrant and she didn't have any wrinkles around the eyes. She wasn't carrying any excess weight. She still had her lovely, long figure and she still gave off that old scent of tantalising femininity. She started working even more in order to improve her situation. She used to slip Bulkhayr's allowance between the pages of his books and she'd leave his meals out in the kitchen for him. On many nights, she'd sneak into his bedroom to study his round, handsome face and the fair beard that had begun to appear against his tawny skin, and she wished more than anything that she could look into his emerald eyes.

Who could be his father? she once asked herself. The question was soul-exhausting because her memory didn't just bring up all those old teenage faces, but also a powerful taste of the dangerous desire she thought she'd long since forgotten, and she could feel herself slipping into its grip once again. She couldn't resist: she masturbated, though her orgasm was mixed with the bitter taste of sin, and it made her swear – not to God – but to the photo of Bulkhayr that hung in her bedroom that she'd never go near the threshold of pleasure again. Then she stuffed a rag in her mouth and heated the cast-iron ladle, which she used to roast coffee until it glowed red. She placed it between her labia and calloused her clitoris and then she passed out from the pain.

That was in the first year of his spurning and with time, she grew used to his silence, learnt to deal with it, and it was enough for her just to know that he was in good health.

When Bulkhayr returned from his trip to Hebariyeh two days later, Farida was sitting by the door of the shed, drying out wreaths of damask roses. She looked up at him and saw that the old unrest had left his face. She couldn't believe her ears when she heard him say, 'Hello,' in a faint voice, clear and full of warmth, and she smiled for the first time in years.

૪ઝ

Buthayna returned, divorced, during the spring vacation in 1989. She arrived at Farida's with two big Versace bags, wearing Dior sunglasses, her hair dyed fair. She raised her sunglasses on her head and her eyes were revealed like crystals, free of wonder, free of sadness. Her round face, her white teeth, her lips a little less red than before, her wide brow, her chest a little more full. In an instant, Bulkhayr recalled every single detail of her body and he waited for any sign from her to signal that they'd indeed had some shared history, but nothing came. He broke out in a cold sweat when she came up and kissed his cheeks. He took in her scent, it was a mix of faint Agarwood coming off her incensed clothes and some new-fangled perfume that smelt of cloves. She seemed to be disguised somehow, or artificial; she'd lost that old fragrance she'd had stored up in her pores. She commented on his height, 'Good lord, you're all grown up now!' and she wasn't exaggerating. She took out a white shirt she'd brought as a gift and said, entirely neutrally, 'I hope it fits.' He took the present indifferently and wondered: could she actually have forgotten? Had what happened between them been real or just some ambiguous escapade he'd embellished in her absence? These Borgesian questions and a creeping doubt engulfed his mind: was his affair with Buthayna just the product of a playful imagination?

His only consolation was that he'd soon find out for sure as she'd come to stay with them – for a month or more – seeing as her own house needed renovating after having been chewed up by waiting and stripped bare by emptiness. In a matter of days, he'd know whether he still had a foothold in her affections. He couldn't go out into the wasteland to clear his head as he usually did, so he went up to the roof, eaten up by his worry and consternation. Could his first love, the one he'd waited and pined for, really be so thick?

He let out a scream for no reason at all up on the roof of the house, confusing the farm animals around him, while below the roof, Buthayna thanked Farida for her hospitality and told her all about what had happened to her in the Emirates.

As soon as she'd got to Dubai, she was struck by the stifling humidity and boredom, the smell of spices and the reek of frying curried fish. 'From the moment I got off the plane it was like that smell was stuck to me. I felt like it was coming from my own body', she explained to Farida. Saloum was gentlemanly and affectionate, but he was never there. He was a faceless husband. A week after she'd arrived in the Emirates from Sarmada, she realized that the emptiness, the loneliness, the confinement, nothing had changed.

Her only task in life was to wait for her husband to return from his job at the school and there was nothing to pass the time except for a few meagre friendships with other teachers' wives. They barely got past small talk, which made the loneliness seem a perfect heaven compared to the constant assault on her privacy and the foolish questions and gossip about every last thing. It was inevitable that she'd keep them all at arm's length. Her days there were written in sentences of words dotted – just to pass the time – with sickly dreams and Saloum was the typical migrant labourer, living by the creed: 'Sun's down, count the cash!'

As the years went by and Saloum al-Rayyash's financial situation began to improve, he was able to open a small restaurant and he would go there to supervise after he was finished teaching for the day. Slowly but surely, they ended up never seeing each other except in passing. Buthayna wasn't demanding, she didn't throw fits. She wasn't the type to moan about her own deterioration, or to complain about anything at all, for that matter. She found ways to mask the void: stringing bead necklaces, honing her old embroidery talents, and watching television, but her womb stayed empty.

She didn't get pregnant and she didn't ask for anything; she was serene and happy to go along in whatever direction life took her.

She docilely accepted her fate every time, but one. 'We have to see a doctor', she told Saloum and so he took her to a women's clinic and they ran some tests. He went back there that evening and returned home with the results.

He delivered the news calmly: 'You're not able to bear children … but that's my fate and I'm not going to gripe about it.' She spent several weeks trying to convince him that he had the right to have a son who'd inherit his bird-cursed family name. They went for a second test, and a third, and every time he came home more loving, but with the same result. She was barren and there was nothing they could do about it. She was even coming around to Saloum's suggestion of adoption when she suddenly had a bout of acute stomach pain and went to see her Iraqi physician, who insisted on running a whole series of tests.

She called Buthayna at home and told her a different truth: 'You could give birth ten times over. Have your husband come and see me.' Despite several long and contentious arguments, Saloum refused to go and submit to any of the doctor's tests and Buthayna realised from his constant foot-dragging that he was the one who was infertile. She gathered up her things and decided she wanted a divorce.

'You know if he'd only told me the truth, hadn't run away from it, I'd have stayed with him. But he lied to me. He lied to me and manipulated me, made me feel more grateful and guilty than I could stand. Everything after that was a lie. Anyway, he didn't put up a fight, he just had one request: that I keep it all a secret because he's afraid of the way people in Sarmada talk.' Buthayna then asked Farida to swear on Bulkhayr's life that she wouldn't tell a soul.

'So what are your plans then?'

'I'm going to go back home! He gave me enough to put my life back together and last a few years without needing anything from anybody. And he promised he'd send what he could.'

The sight of her smooth, ample body hit him like a full-scale military attack and his erection was killing him. Nothing, absolutely nothing else mattered. He didn't miss a single chance to touch her. He used to surprise her when she was stood at the sink; he'd rub the back of his hand over her arse and disappear before she'd even turned around.

Three-quarters of his day was spent prisoner to an erection that just wouldn't abate. He watched her, when she moved and when she was still, but his eyes wouldn't meet hers. He tried his hardest to stop, but it seemed there was nothing he could do. It happened again and again: he barged in on her, pressed himself up against her; he didn't miss a single chance to get close to her flesh.

She found it distressing at first, but she never tried to tell Farida. She pushed him away with all her insistence and might, but there was some satiny contentment muffling her fears, something tickling about the dangerous game played by a divorcee in her thirties and an adolescent on the verge of sixteen. He rubbed at the bristly edges of her empty days, tempted sin, kindled her memory and lack, and somehow this put her at ease, kept her from confronting him. She blamed herself. She blamed her soul. She was even more anxious to see how renovation on the house was coming along and she paid the workers more to finish the job quickly. She was worried she might grow weak. She didn't want to venture down that path with an unruly teenager as it would only further confuse her already traumatised spirit.

She snapped at him the next time he grabbed her arse as she was sweeping the floor. He'd squeezed her harder than usual and it made her nervous. This was something she hadn't seen coming. He'd let her get used to the light touches that left no trace; giving her a shiver and disappearing in the blink of an eye, but it was different this time.

'Bulkhayr, stop it! I need to talk to you.' He stopped and turned to look at her. 'Next time you touch me, I'm going to cut off your hand. The only reason I put up with you is because I know you're going through a hard time right now. Do you understand me?'

He stood there, trembling, and as she stared into his eyes, she couldn't help but pity this being who was being tortured by his own body. His eyes welled up: 'Forgive me, Auntie', he said, crushingly.

'You're forgiven', she said and turned around, abandoning him to new bouts of devastating anxiety.

Those fantasies had been with him for many years and they would come to him every once in a while. He was chronically frustrated, storm-battered by his body, which swept away all wisdom before it and knocked him down over and over again. He lost the brittle peace he'd got from Hebariyeh. Unabashed desire fled its confines and became his overriding concern, his focus, his constant preoccupation. He couldn't concentrate on anything and his thoughts were filled with all the women he knew, kin and non-kin. He made a hole in the bathroom door, forgetting his plea for forgiveness, and invaded her private nudity, panicked lest Farida should sneak up and catch him as he watched. Nevertheless, the longing he felt for the sight of her naked body fixed his eye to the hole as he watched her undress. He watched as she muttered a few prayers and the name of God, before pouring the water over her body and rubbing herself with laurel soap. She, too, was thirsty with want and loneliness and tormented by the pleas of a body that wouldn't die down.

When she spotted the peephole, her face flushed with anger and she fought back an explosion of anger. She slapped her clothes on and bolted from the bathroom: 'What do you say I tell Farida what a little bastard you are?'

'Whatever. I don't give a damn', he answered with wounded pride. 'I need you and it's killing me.'

She didn't know what to say to that. She could feel her last line of defences beginning to crumble under the pressure of his caddish insistence. 'You're nuts. I'm like your mother, kid', she said, looking into his emerald eyes, knitting her arched eyebrows, squinting as her own dark eyes filled with disappointment and pique.

'But my mother didn't feed me molasses when I was little,' he said with defiant cheek. 'All my mother ever did was feed me shit and bring me into this whore of a world.' And then he stormed out and slammed the front door behind him.

He went into the wasteland for three days, spending the night in the basalt caves, walking among the rocks, imitating the howls and shrieks of the wolves and wild dogs. With the arrival of spring, the rugged wasteland had become some kind of miracle for the eyes. The sky was suddenly gloomy with spring clouds and in the west, a storm began raining down while the sun still shone on the eastern part of the rocky tract. He felt bliss pricking his face – a velvety drizzle washing his loneliness. He stripped off his clothes and stood there naked, spreading his arms to the rain, as the sunlight that fell across his body was washed with drops of purest water. Two jackals hid behind a rock in the distance and watched sceptically as this naked human and his two sizable penises were washed by the sky.

Farida told Buthayna about the torture he'd put her through, how he used to greet her with a heart-wrenching silence. She told her how she was willing to give her life for him, but that she didn't know what to do. 'He won't talk to anybody anymore. He doesn't relate to anyone. It breaks my heart. Every time he goes out into the wasteland, I count the days he's gone by the minute. I can't stop him, I can't talk to him. When he comes home, he locks himself in his bedroom and he just reads and reads for days. Sometimes he'll go two days without even eating.' She confessed to Buthayna that the Epistles of Wisdom had helped her and that she'd put her fate in God's hands – she'd even swapped her old diaphanous, fine lace headscarf for a thicker one to signal her increased piety – and that the only thing that settled her soul was reading the Blessed Epistles and also how she'd cauterised her desire with the searing iron ladle. The only good news was that business was booming and she'd been able to an add an extra room to the shed, which was where Buthayna slept.

When Bulkhayr returned home, he disappeared into his silence, leaving the women to whisper the secrets of their hearts to each other. There was a knock at the door: it was a warning about his school absences and that he was in danger of being expelled if his truancy continued. He tore up the warning, not minding the messenger who'd delivered it, and slammed the door in his face. He went into his room, picked up a dingy book and began cutting the leaves with a ruler. The book was a biography of 'Rimbaud, the vagabond poet' told grippingly by Sidqi Ismaeel. To Bulkhayr, just the name Arthur Rimbaud sounded thrilling and he could feel it every time he read anything by him or about him. He devoured the book in one evening and then he read it again the next day. There was some sort of life force coming from the poet's death so to get it out of his head he picked up the novel *Madeleine, or Beneath the Linden Trees* by Alphonse Karr as adapted by Mustafa Lutfi al-Manfaluti, and for the first time in his life, something he'd read brought tears to his eyes. He was sobbing when she came into the room. She saw him reading, the tears staining his face, but he hadn't noticed her come in. She hesitated at first, and then she stepped forward. 'What's wrong? Why are you crying?'

He looked up and quickly wiped the tears from his face. 'Nothing. It's nothing, I've just got something in my eye.' She ran her hand through his carob-coloured hair. She wanted to embrace him, to squeeze him against her chest, to drown him in the abundance of her soul, the springs of her compassion. But she did nothing of the sort.

She merely ran her hands through his hair and whispered hoarsely, 'I want you to know you're my everything.'

She didn't lock her bedroom door as she did every other night to forestall his rash offences, she just slipped into bed after she'd perfumed herself and dressed in a thin slip. Her heart beat a drum of anticipation. He opened the door slowly and she shut her eyes, pretending to be asleep, as the faint glow of the nightlight fell across her face. He moved toward her on tiptoe and slid under the blanket into bed, settling behind her without touching her. She could hear him panting. He reached his hand out and placed it on her shoulder, and then he moved it up to her hair, rubbing it, inhaling the long-awaited scent. She let him, she didn't want to startle him. He brought his hand to her lolling breast as she tried to breathe regularly, pretending to sleep, while his hands woke every dormant cell of her smooth and sculpted body. When he tweaked her nipple, she pushed his hand away with faux-annoyance and turned to face him. 'What do you think you're doing, kid?' she whispered.

'I've missed you.' His lips moved as if in prayer and his hands fell silent as if in preparation for another set of bodily devotions, as if gathering all their strength before invading seduction's lairs. She rolled over onto her back and he covered her lips with his own and in their untameable kiss, saliva poured daintily from mouth to mouth, mixed and their bodies lit up. Hands were untied from dewy memories and set free to roam among the resplendent, gushing gardens of her body. His fingers began to climb up her ivory thighs like a flock of hungry goats, jumping excitedly over her grassy plain, rubbing with the calm deliberation of a seasoned reaper; slipping past her labia down into the hot liquid valley, and then gliding over her excited clitoris.

She grabbed his hand. She was determined to stop him; he'd gone way past the limits of what she'd wanted, and quickly. She thought it would be a romantic night: that he would encounter some of her body and a lot of love's whisper. She could never have imagined how bold and rash he'd be. She was about to push him away and jump out of bed, when he whispered with all the longing in the world, 'I'm begging you: let me put my hand there.'

All her defences collapsed in a single moment under the hail of that reckless torrent of emotion, that passion. This was a moment that would never be repeated, she thought, as she held his hand back – a moment that would mark the rest of her days forever. The fire would consume her unless she put a stop to this foolishness.

Desire won out, that howling anticipation in her hand as she waited for his youthful fingers to feed her his flesh and his blood and his heat. Rather than push him away, she wrapped her hand around his and eased it back down into her moist sex. She gave him free reign over all those remaining spaces without obstacle or reservation, and in a voice that resembled a pure spring, she whispered, 'Don't burn me with your fire', borrowing a line from an Egyptian film she'd seen in the Emirates.

His hand would learn the meaning of moisture in bloom; it would discover the secret of woman's dew. Her hand would reach out to grasp his animal erection and when it did, the shock of two penises made her shiver. She stopped everything. 'Wait a second, wait a second', she whispered, sitting up. She wanted to see what she'd felt so she threw off the covers and pulled down his pyjamas and her heart almost froze when she saw them, sticking up, pulsing together. She took them in her hands and tried to stifle her giggling, and then she was overcome with an insane lust. She must've come a dozen times and almost fell to pieces from the constant trembling. He only noticed because she was moaning beneath him; he had one of his penises inside of her and the other rubbing against her, nearly reaching her navel. 'Don't come inside me. Don't come ins …'

Her night had clearly drifted toward the epitome of forbidden bliss. There was too much fragile stealth and the body opened wide to its farthest possible limits. She took him into the bathroom with her, defying any latent fear that they might be caught in the act. She bathed him: scrubbed him like a child and soaped up his two slender penises. Then she squeezed toothpaste onto them and massaged them with water and he could feel all his apprehensions diffusing mintily in the desire-sated air. It was like a rite of worship. She knew that the pleasure she'd experienced was unlike anything a woman could ever hope to attain and that it would be silly to give up this immense gift no matter what the justification. She kneeled down at his feet and began to kiss them, nibbling at the two heads, taking one into her mouth and sucking it, while her hand milked the other. She brought them to climax and he knew he was about to come and tugged at her hair, but she clung to him and he came. She swallowed. She licked at them and took them in her silky mouth, washing away his semen, like the placenta of an animal that had just given birth, until they died down between her lips. He looked down at her, his face marked by a few red spots, and watched her ministrations, grinning like a lizard basking in the sun after a downpour. He was nodding in one continuous, harmonious movement and then her voice brought him back to dreadful reality.

'Did you enjoy that, you little pimp?'

On the other side of the door, eavesdropping Farida held back her tears and then skulked, broken, back to her bedroom. She wept silently until her anger was exhausted, and she submitted to all that had happened without daring to confront them.

ॐ

He was beaming. Buthayna had set him alight, given him something besides solitude, and they started doing it every chance they got. They were drunk on a bottomless love. They started avoiding Farida whose face had begun to contort with the signs of devotion to God, faith and the holy books. She was constantly going to the majlis to worship and tidy up, tending the carpets and the candles and the incense. It was like her second home. She was escaping from what she knew was going on in the shed, from an atmosphere heavy with desire, and old feelings that roared to life when she recalled them, after a month of madness and burning lust, and then Buthayna's house was ready.

They had more freedom now. Although they'd lost the pleasure of stolen moments, they were able to open their relationship up to manic lust. He went to see her every day and would occasionally stay over for three nights straight. Nothing kept him from visiting except for a sudden impulse to go out into the wasteland and howl, or the compulsion to read a new book, as well as his learning how to drink arak. He occasionally put on his school uniform: fatigues with a tenth-grade insignia, and set off – not to school – but rather out into the wasteland to clear his head and hone his body on the unique basalt and its radiant energy.

After six months and with the beginning of the eleventh grade, his passion began to fade. Buthayna could see he was constantly lost in thought, intermittently silent and distracted; he was more interested in drink and drunkenness than in her. He began repeating phrases and poems, and passages that she didn't understand at all; it seemed as if he was suddenly bored with everything. He was no longer the lusty teenager he'd been – the rocky stud. He was more tender and liable to be hurt by words. She didn't know what to do about him: the further he drifted, the more she craved him.

She finally realised her dilemma: she was used to the idea of a foolish, doomed romance. She'd been certain that he'd grow up and leave her, but she'd always figured it'd be some girl his age who'd decimate him with her charms. She never dreamt that she'd lose him to a lusty old weirdo called Arthur Rimbaud, who seemed to spout never-ending nonsense!

Meanwhile, his mother was heading down an entirely different path: a shaykh, who was a great scholar of the secrets of the Epistles of Wisdom, had proposed a Seeing Marriage to her, which was a kind of marriage between a Druze man and a Druze woman who would be companions in every regard except that their relationship would remain entirely celibate. They would share the burdens of daily life and the secrets of the faith and immerse themselves in the spiritual together, renouncing the body, suppressing the self and its fire with their cool reason, in order to achieve knowledge of the true self and the universal intellect on an eternal journey toward the distant essence within each human being.

She knew she had to ask him what he thought, but he just snorted and said, 'Do whatever you want. I don't care.' He sank back into the gloom of his own private meditation. The words of the wild French teenager and his call to tear down the senses in order to create a new vision filled him with terror. The mysterious sentiments transmitted by a soul convulsed with a wisdom induced by dread made him feel as if he needed a new alphabet – a new exploding, exotic language that had roamed the expanses of instinct. He wanted to know who this person was whom he was accompanying; he wanted to know his soul and his body before they'd been tamed.

He felt Rimbaud's translated soul pushing through the sophistry of vague pronouncements, flashing in his moist, raw insides. He touched lights that would open up to him in his own mind's eye in the form of golden roosters crowing for promised dawns, which the sky sent down in floods of wine. He felt he had everything and that his mind was expanding widely, pushing him beyond his narrow confines and the ordered world of Sarmada. He saw that he would need a new language in order to realize his desires, so he started to learn French. The letters didn't curve and swoop like Arabic letters, they didn't have the same explosive force that comes from dotting. Arabic letters are arched and pliant. They can bend and twist in a way that other scripts can't. The letters in French were open; they had no sanctity, no great secrets, but still they unlocked new horizons and new lands that he couldn't even believe existed, and it made him smile whenever he said them. His mouth would gape, making it seem as if his scowling face had been wrenched open. Not to mention that this was the distant and seductive colonial voice, and yet he couldn't quite understand how it could be that French imperialism had left nothing behind except for a few words, which had crept into their daily conversation, unlike in Lebanon or the Maghreb. As he repeated the French words into the voice recorder, he discovered that speaking French made people look as if they were always smiling or, what was more likely, that they were telling a joke so you could never tell when they were being serious.

It was something Arthur Rimbaud had said – or had he said it? It was hard to know anymore: 'the body a treasure to waste'. Buthayna didn't get it; she thought it went too far. She knew that all she wanted was for the body of this tanned adolescent to extinguish partially the thirst of her own unique body and its ardent rhythm. But he had another passion in his life and it was tugging him away.

The words he'd learnt on Buthayna's body as a child still stung with desire and molasses after all those years, for he was the only student in the world who'd learnt to read and write with his other senses. The words themselves began to enchant him, to steal him from Buthayna's embrace. She could never have imagined that her teenage lover would sink into her, perfumed with book dust, repeating strange words in her ear. Then once when he broke out in a raving fantasy, she realised she hadn't anticipated any of it and that she was beginning to lose control. She was no longer the older guide whom the crazy young man had seduced and whose parched heart he'd then scorched, and yet she was comforted by the vague assurance that no woman on earth could have resisted going to the furthest limits of madness if they'd met this alluring rake. He was bursting with wicked ruinous lust and a devilish passion that couldn't be resisted.

These thoughts came to her as she lay there, completely naked, wading through a mire of unease as he melted bars of chocolate in a copper coffee pot over the leaping blue flame of her gas stove. He brought the coffee pot over to her and dipped his finger into the hot dark liquid. He began to drizzle the chocolate onto her lambent-white belly as her body seized in pleasure and pain. He traced the burning dark-chocolate letters of the French alphabet across her polished, twitching skin, and when he'd finished writing out the vowels, he leaned to lick them off. Old memories were brought to mind and new ones were forged as he licked the chocolate off her body and then he whispered to her, 'Did you know that letters have sounds and scents?' She laughed at his inappropriately timed linguistic theories, which broke in and interrupted her pleasure.

He stopped his licking and recited a poem by Rimbaud on vowels that he'd memorised in translation.

'A: Black, E: White, I: Red, U: Green, O: Blue, the vowels.
One day, I'll explain your coming births:
A, black velvet coat of gleaming flies
that buzz and dive round heartless smells,
Gaping shadows; E, innocence of steam and tents,
proud glacier spears, white kings, shudder of ombelles;
I, crimson, spewed blood, smile on lovely lips
whether enraged or remorsefully drunk;
U, sine, the divine oscillation of turquoise seas,
the peace of beast filled pastures, the peace of wrinkles
which alchemy stamps on wide and bookish brows;
O, transcendent Trumpet, chirring strangely,
Silences crossed by Worlds and Angels:
– O, Omega, the violet ray shining out His Eyes! –

He recited, as he stretched out beside her, how the poet had tried to give the letters new meanings, images, spice-tastes, lights and colours.

'I don't understand a word,' she said coquettishly revolted. She moved closer to nibble at the bottom of his neck and lick his lips, but he pushed her away roughly.

'You know, all we ever do is sleep together and you're always making different noises, especially when you're coming like, "Ahhhhhhhh", or sometimes "Ee ee ee ee ee." Lots of times you just say, "Yes! Yes! Yes! Yes!" Can you explain what they all mean?'

'Stop it! Shame on you. You're embarrassing me.'

'Seriously, tell me. What makes all those sounds different? Isn't it weird that you can make those noises when you're panting and you know exactly what they mean, but then when we write them down and read them off your body, all of a sudden you can't understand? I swear you'll never understand a bloody thing!'

She held back her laughter when she saw he was being serious and that his questions had been meant to mock the limits of her comprehension. She tried to stop him, but he knocked the glass of arak back. He stood up, still completely naked, and started spouting the words of someone a lot older than he was, gesturing and making faces, as if he were in front of some notional audience. 'They're the first sounds: nature's unadulterated sonata. They're called "vowels" because they're in all the vows us sick people make. They're there in the first cries of birth, they're there in our last screams of pleasure. They're what give us everything pure and clean. They're how we get terror, and fear, and lust, and pain – the will to stay. They're the vocal code to reproduction. If we can unlock their meanings, we'll be able to explore the secret of humanity, the depths of our first language, when everyone used to make the exact same sounds to talk about precise and unambiguous things, which didn't have names most of the time, but could be felt – sensed.

'Rimbaud tried to capture them, to categorise them, to give the alphabet back its glory. But the problem was that his language was holding him back. French was too narrow for his passion and that's why he had to break away from it. Yes, he broke away from his language. He tried to invent a new language in which the words had scents and characters. He gave them shapes and colours they'd never had before but French didn't help him. That's the real secret behind his silence: his language couldn't contain his soul.

'After he'd destroyed his senses, his experiences could no longer be expressed in words. If he'd known Arabic at the time, he could've invented a new sacred alphabet and become a prophet in the East. Rimbaud wanted to be a son of the sun so he studied Eastern wisdom, the spring and the source. He went to search for another explosive energy, preserved in language, in the letters themselves. He had a hunch that it was here, in the East, in our language, in its magic and mystery and shades. That's why he abandoned poetry once he'd used it to get rid of all the toxins he'd inherited from his forefathers over millennia, and slipped off to go look for a different kind of meaning – something less dangerous than words. He exposed what mankind has always tried to stamp out. He straightened it out. He strangled it. He extracted all the deep longing for freedom, for an awesome trust between life and one's self, for contact with the great poetic being, the creator of the world.'

Her jaw dropped as she peered into his clouded eyes and watched them become black as he let out a flood of words and thoughts. She was worried about him as he stood there, sweating, speaking – not to her – but as if to someone else. His thin, naked body moved about the room and he spoke hurriedly as if he were reading from tablets and ideas he couldn't see with his eyes, which were caked with too much sadness and earnest. It was an unimaginable and illuminating moment and it was then that he began to be aware of the threads running through his life.

She was struck by his ideas. It threw everything she knew into doubt. It yanked her from the complacency of her intellect and femininity and she felt like slapping him, or hitting him, anything to stop this lunacy. But then, before she could even reply, he left; he left her there naked and decorated with French chocolate vowels. He gathered up his books and notebooks and walked out. She felt a sin-tinged remorse for those times she'd made him learn to write the letters with his tongue and taste them with his lips. She felt that she'd finally come to the last chapter of the transgression that still tormented her. She decided that she quickly had to regain her real life, to return to her senses, but there was still something vague that gnawed at her, that wore her out. She desperately wanted him to come back one last time, to pull off the final grand lark that had been too long in coming.

He began to drift further and further away, even to run away from her. The roles in their old struggle were now reversed and now instead of her fleeing his constant harassment, it was him running from her, sinking deeper into a thrilling world of words brought to life in the pages of the devil's books – that was Rimbaud's nickname. Could words really have such power? She knew that magicians used talismans to get the genies to submit and to serve, and that repeating certain words could bring on disasters or stave them off, but she'd never entirely believed in those myths; even back when she'd gone to visit the soothsayer of Kanakir. She watched her little one, her sweetheart, the companion of her loneliness and the quencher of her thirst, the giver of meaning and bringer of light. She could see him departing her bodily heaven for a wordy hell. She was tormented by worry for her boy and she felt indescribably guilty. Despite the premonitions of danger and the distress that left her lovely face ashen, she decided with uncommon intelligence not to object, but rather to go along with this lunacy. It was nothing more than a youthful fit; one taste of molasses was all it would take to bring him back from his chocolate fit. She took comfort in her reasoning: he had to be allowed to taste another flavour before he could realise the value of what he had. But away from the body and its logic, her heart was still in thrall to that sixteen-year-old boy whose eyes had turned black.

It just isn't fair that we're forced to wear out our trousers on the chairs at school. Yes, it was most likely Rimbaud who'd given him the idea that school was the exact opposite of what his heart required. He longed for the chance to flee far away, somewhere outside this thicket that annihilated every last desire. In the translated melodies of Rimbaud's poems, he found his devotion and his course. It would lead him through life, on his intoxicated quest for great answers. He copied out Rimbaud's French expression: 'Yes, I've shut my eyes to your light, and you are all phony negroes.'

A peculiar energy filled his soul. School was the most deathbed place in his life and home was a wide grave. The village on the mountain edge was drowning in its eternal silence and amazement, colluding in its historical fate, turning into a chicken coop on the farm of the nation. He had no reason to stay.

One early morning, he woke up, quietly and calmly, and went into his mother's room where he stole a thousand lire from her handbag. He packed a small bag with some pointless things, put on his shoes, and walked out of Sarmada in the direction of Damascus, where he would eventually fall into a hysterical madness that no one would ever hear about.

He never returned to Sarmada except for the evening on the day Farida was buried. He came limping on an artificial leg, sallow-faced and weighed down by a crushing emptiness that no human being could hope to bear.

༄

So it was up to me to put an end to the shedding of Sarmada's memory and put all the pieces together. I, Rafi Azmi, came to Sarmada a few days ago to discover a village that I hadn't known and stories I'd never heard before – or as I've been told, stories I hadn't listened to well enough the first time. It's up to me to conclude things, to stop writing the stories if only because otherwise they'll never end, and to make a quick round past everyone to make sure they've played their parts and left, or to discover that they're still waiting, ready to fill in any odd role.

Buthayna had a breakdown after Bulkhayr left. A few weeks later, she went to visit Farida and her new husband at the shed and asked if she could go into his room. She breathed in his scent and took some of his clothes. She cried that he'd gone away and she knew that she'd lost him forever. Before she left, she spotted the chest that she'd been given by the soothsayer of Kanakir. She pulled it out from under a pile of books and asked Farida if she could have it back. Without waiting to hear the answer, she left, taking the chest home with her.

At home, after a second bout of mourning and smelling his

clothes, she broke the lock on the chest and took out leaves of the book *al-Azif*. She looked through it. She examined the drawings and symbols and letters and words. She felt as if the words were destroying her and she surged with anger. She took the sheets and used them to light a fire. The villagers tried desperately to put it out, but there was no use and the blaze and its fiery tongues burnt all night, turning the house to ashes. There was no trace of her body. That fire was like a prophecy that would burn the place and usher it to its rebirth, although no one knew when. On that flaming night, the full Sarmadan moon glowed a fiery red, as if it were a keyhole or a magic eye through the heavenly gate.

The Shaykh found he couldn't bear being married to Farida, not as if they were sister and brother at least, and so he ran away to the monastic isolation of the mountains to safeguard the oath he'd sworn to uphold. He wore himself out with hard labour and lashed his back with a whip, which he'd made himself out of electrical cables, in the hope that pain and punishment would kill the desire he'd failed to suppress. Farida, for her part, locked herself up in the shed after the divorce.

She locked herself away just as her mother-in-law Umm Salman had done years before and her breasts began to grow larger and larger, transforming her suppressed desires into green breast milk. Then she suddenly had the realisation that most of those special herbs that were prescribed to promote the production of breast milk and treat despair were nothing more than dried-up opium and poppy. Then she sliced her nipples open and out flowed blood mixed in with the green milk, which she bottled and stored with her straw.

She devoted herself entirely to contemplation, silence and prayer, and fell deep down into a well of forgetting until this very evening.

Salama found the bottles so he brought them back to his house and asked me what I thought he should do with them.

Today was the day I heard a voice announcing her death over

the loud-speaker. The people of Sarmada ran over and improvised an abbreviated funeral but the shaykhs refused to pray over her body. I felt that I'd got Sarmada back and that I was finally finished with it, all in the same moment, and that it was time for me to leave.

I said goodbye to Salama without giving him an answer about the bottles of milk and was preparing to leave. I turned on my mobile and called my boss in Dubai to tell him that I'd be in Damascus by tomorrow and that I'd make up all the work I'd missed. I looked to see if there were any messages from Paris, but there weren't. I called Dr Azza several times but her phone was turned off. I had the feeling that I never wanted to see her again, or even speak to her. I would just publish everything I'd recorded and send her a copy. There wasn't anything I could tell her.

Just as I was coming around to this surprising outcome, a stolid man with an artificial leg walked up. I swear to God he looked like Long John Silver from Treasure Island, the children's book. I nearly broke out in a smile as he got closer and it occurred to me that all he was missing was a parrot. As I studied him, I could see that he was an expert at ignoring and paying no attention to questioning eyes. He was that rare breed of human being: dignified and mysterious, but spirited nonetheless.

He greeted Salama by name and then asked, 'Where did you bury her?'

Salama pointed him in the direction of the grave, outside the village limits, and told the inscrutable stranger that he was planning to move the body to al-Manabi, Farida's hometown. The man left him and headed toward the shed.

Outside a crowd of villagers had gathered, in a quiet curious circle, interrupted by repeated whispers: 'It's Bulkhayr, Farida's son!'

He came out a little while later carrying an old, carefully knotted bundle and walked up to Salama. 'Did you wrap her in a winding sheet?' he asked bitterly. Salama's head drooped sadly and he leaned down to pick up his shovel and walked off, without answering.

Bulkhayr unwrapped the bundle in front of the silent crowd and took out a wooden toy wrapped in old rags, a jar of kohl, a bottle of perfume, a toothbrush, a triangular amulet, perfumed Fa soap and a neatly folded, white veil. He unfolded the veil and held it up in front of the crowd. It was embroidered with coloured buttons of different sizes: shirt buttons lined up all around the edge and beneath each button, she'd sewn the name of its owner. Some were two-holed, others had four holes, in the chaotic order of that bright white winding sheet, which began to shine and glimmer in the fading sunlight. The voices began quietly at first, and then slowly grew louder and louder: 'God rest her soul! God rest her soul! God rest her soul!'